PLANTS *for all* SEASONS

PLANTS
for all
SEASONS

250 PLANTS FOR YEAR-ROUND SUCCESS
IN YOUR GARDEN

Andrew Lawson

FRANCES LINCOLN

For Rosemary Verey, who opened my eyes to so many things

HALF TITLE PAGE
Allium christophii in summer

TITLE PAGE
An apple tree in midsummer has
been brought to life by an underplanting of self-seeding blue
Campanula persicifolia and by sprays of
the rambler rose 'Paul's Himalayan
Musk', trained into the tree.

LEFT
Lunaria annua 'Alba Variegata' earns
its place in the spring with a show
of flowers that coincides with late
tulips. In autumn it extends armfuls
of coin-shaped seedpods that glow
silver in the low winter light,
adding a touch of brilliance to the
garden through the darkest months
of the year.

Frances Lincoln Ltd
4 Torriano Mews, Torriano Avenue, London NW5 2RZ

Plants for all Seasons
Copyright © Frances Lincoln Limited 1992
Text and photographs copyright © Andrew Lawson 1992

British Library Cataloguing in Publication Data
A catalogue record for this book
is available from the British Library

First Frances Lincoln Edition: 1992
First Frances Lincoln paperback edition: 1999

ISBN 0 7112 1392 5

Set in 11/13pt Perpetua by SX Composing DTP
Printed and bound in Hong Kong

3 5 7 9 8 6 4 2

CONTENTS

CHOOSING PLANTS FOR A LASTING DISPLAY

Space is at a premium in most gardens. There are many gardeners who would like to grow more plants than their gardens can accommodate, and most of us would also like to extend the period in which our gardens look good. One of the best ways to get the most out of limited space is to grow plants that perform in more than one season. Among these will be a few that earn their keep all the year round.

Unfortunately, some of the most spectacular garden plants have only a single season of display. A tree or shrub that produces blossom for just one glorious week in spring might give you intense pleasure for that short time – but you will be lucky if it does not rain that week, and of course you must not take a holiday or you will miss it altogether. For the rest of the year the plant will be a passenger in your garden. In this category of short-season plants I would put shrubs like forsythia and some – but not all – of the flowering cherries.

You will get better value from your garden if, for the majority of your plantings, you select plants that have a dual purpose and, better still, some that look attractive all through the year. You can find trees (including flowering cherries) that have magnificent autumn colour in addition to the more ephemeral show of blossom in the spring. Some produce eye-catching fruits that follow a good display of flowers. Others have colourful bark that is of interest all year but particularly in winter, when their principal attraction, the foliage, is absent.

Among the tens of thousands of shrubs and perennials available, some of the most valuable are those that flower more or less continuously across the seasons. They include the perennial wallflower *Erysimum* 'Bowles' Mauve', which is colourful for all

Dominating a border in late spring, *Euphorbia characias* ssp. *wulfenii* makes a good companion for tulips, cowslips, forget-me-nots, and the golden young foliage of *Spiraea japonica* 'Goldflame'. A few weeks later, when this spring flush is over, the euphorbia flowers will still be in action to accompany the purple-flowered *Geranium* × *magnificum* growing around its base, and the blue *Geranium* 'Johnson's Blue' beside the spiraea. The euphorbia is useful not only on account of its long flowering season, but also for the unostentatious lime-green colour of its flowers, which look good in association with almost any other colour.

twelve months in a good year. Others can be found among the roses: 'Iceberg', for instance, has its first flush of bloom in midsummer but is still in action in early winter.

Winter is a testing time for the gardener. Admittedly it may be a season when you do not often want to potter around outside, but even the view out of a window will be bleak indeed if there is nothing of interest in the garden. Many plants have second strings to their bow for winter colour and form. Fruits and berries and colourful bark and stems are obvious examples, but you should also be aware of the possibilities of seedheads, dried flowers and even the dead foliage of plants like grasses. If you have ever seen the lovely effect of frost on clumps of the tall grass *Miscanthus sinensis*, then you will resist the temptation to be over-zealous when tidying up the garden in the autumn. Plants that die gracefully are a great asset and will populate your winter garden with companionable ghosts. And there is always plenty of bounty to spare for the indoor winter flower arrangement, which can be a *compôte* of dried fruits and seedheads, leaves and coloured stems in addition to the more traditional everlasting flowers.

RIGHT The tall grass *Miscanthus sinensis* 'Strictus' makes an effective backcloth for a clump of the autumn-flowering daisy *Aster amellus* 'King George'. Within two months (OPPOSITE LEFT) winter has reduced both perennials to whispering skeletons. The plants are dead above ground level and could have been cleared in a late-autumn purge of the borders, but it is a much better idea to let them decline in their own time. Dead foliage and seedheads give your borders an extra season of interest. In cold weather the plant skeletons provide a framework on which the frost builds a filigree of silver and white. There is also a practical reason for leaving the clearing of borders to the early spring: dead foliage acts as a blanket, and gives the growth some protection from the worst of the cold weather.

ABOVE A border ablaze in autumn with *Cotinus* 'Flame'. This specimen has remained unpruned for several years, and has reached the size of a small tree. If it had been regularly pruned the autumn colour would be even more spectacular, as the young wood of cotinus bears larger leaves. However, there is a down side to pruning, as it prevents the plant from flowering. Unpruned, this cotinus flowers copiously in summer, with the fluffy flower heads that give the shrub its name of 'smoke bush'.

The evergreen background

Winter is a test too for the design of your garden. Walls, paths, steps and other structural features such as pergolas and arbours take on a new prominence when stripped of their cosmetic decoration of flowers and foliage. This is where the evergreen plants come into their own. A few well-shaped evergreens at strategic points in the garden will keep the show going through the long, difficult months. A framework of clipped evergreen hedges and screens draws graphic patterns in the winter garden, especially when it is dusted with an overlay of snow and viewed from the comfort of the house.

As a rule, the evergreens tend to be slow-growing and long-lived and so they are ideal for providing the living backbone of the garden. Although many – mahonia and holly, for instance – have brittle leaves, giving rather a hard overall texture, there are a few, like choisya, that have soft and shapely foliage. The conifers are a natural choice to provide some evergreen interest in the garden, though as most of them change so little over the year they seem rather lifeless compared with the majority of garden plants, which respond so interestingly to the seasons. It is as well to mix them with foliage plants of a softer texture to relieve their rather rigid effect.

'Evergreen' is hardly the right word for plants with winter foliage that is colourful but far from green. I am thinking, for instance, of that invaluable plant for hedges, the beech, which has leaves that go russet in autumn and remain on the hedge until they are pushed off by the fresh new growth of spring. And in some of the variegated 'evergreens' – the hollies and ivies among them – patterns of white, cream or yellow decorate the green background of the leaves and in some cases almost obliterate it altogether. Bright-toned foliage of this kind can be a welcome relief from the worthy but sometimes dull dark leaves of the true evergreens.

The evergreen framework of this garden ensures that it remains interesting all the year round. The pair of stepped box hedges will look much the same through the seasons, as will the yew structures – hedges topped with topiary and obelisks with square bases. Creating an evergreen structure of this quality demands up to ten years of hard work and patience, but the reward is a consistent effect that should last for many decades if the evergreens are properly maintained.

Plants that spread and seed themselves

Annuals and biennials are long-lasting in rather a different way. Although they have a relatively short life – and certainly the individual flowers may be very short-lived – these plants will seed themselves with abandon, often appearing where you least expect them.

One of the sea hollies, *Eryngium giganteum*, is known charmingly as 'Miss Willmott's ghost'. The English gardener Ellen Ann Willmott (1858–1934) used to scatter seeds of this plant in every garden she visited. The plant soon established itself in these gardens by seeding itself in subsequent years. The descendants of Miss Willmott's seeds survive still in many a garden – her ghost lives on.

It is said that you can judge the age of a wild hedgerow by counting the number of species of tree that have taken root there. Rather the same sort of rule applies to gardens. You can judge the maturity of a garden by the number of plants that have arrived more or less by chance, and have been allowed to remain. Stray plants, seeding themselves in cracks in a stone terrace or in crevices in a wall, bring mellowness to a garden, softening the hard edges of the design, and filling out the bare areas that inevitably appear as the seasons draw on.

The distinction between uninvited weeds and welcome self-seeders is a fine one. A self-seeding plant in the wrong place becomes a weed and should be rooted out. None of them are difficult to remove, although many are so prolific that they have to be taken out in large numbers to prevent them from overrunning the garden. The virtue of these plants is that they are expendable. And their cultivation is the easiest form of gardening, because it is passive. You do nothing to encourage self-seeders to grow, but merely remove them when they are out of place.

Not many of the self-seeding plants will be stocked at your local nursery or garden centre.

Perennials like valerian and *Corydalis lutea* and biennials such as honesty and the Welsh poppy are often regarded as too common to be worth selling. They are not all available from seed merchants either. Firms tend to specialize in plants that are difficult to grow, so that you have to keep coming back to them for more. Plants that go on for ever are, in marketing terms, like the everlasting light bulb – a product that is so successful it is bad for business. There is nothing else for it. You will have to cultivate a friendship with Ellen Willmott's descendants, and invite them to your garden.

LEFT The daisy *Erigeron karvinskianus* has found its way into this well-populated terrace by self-seeding among helianthemums and hellebores, artfully planted in gaps between the stones.

RIGHT A controlled plot of self-seeders. Spilling on to a gravel path, clumps of white and purple honesty (*Lunaria annua*) rise above a carpet of self-sown forget-me-nots (*Myosotis*), with the Welsh poppy (*Meconopsis cambrica*) providing a flash of contrasting yellow. Young wild daisy plants and self-seeded foxgloves (*Digitalis purpurea*) are poised to take over the scene a few weeks later.

Underplanting and ground cover

It can be helpful to think of a garden as composed of three distinct horizontal layers, although these layers are usually blurred by the intermingling of the plants. The top layer is composed of the trees. Most of them are perched on standard stems, leaving room for the middle layer – of shrubs and perennials – to merge below. At the lowest level, creeping and ground-hugging plants can be used as ground cover to fill any remaining gaps between the plants – assuming, of course, that the gardener wants every scrap of the ground to be covered. Some gardeners like to look upon each plant as a specimen to be enjoyed in a degree of isolation from its neighbours. In this context ground-covering plants can be an interference. In my own garden, however, I regard any patch of bare ground as a failure on my part, at least in summer. Some gardeners, myself included, seem to be driven by a moral imperative to hide the ground and draw a skirt around the bases of shrubs, rather as our nineteenth-century ancestors covered the legs of pianos, which were otherwise considered rather naughty. In practice the selection of plants for this lowest layer can make a great contribution to the overall effect of the garden.

The feet of shrubs and trees are usually densely shaded and the best ground-cover plants need to be not only shade-lovers but also coloured in such a way that they will shine out of the gloom. The variegated lamiums are ideal in this respect, with their silver-patterned foliage that sparkles with light. The variegated periwinkles are good for covering large areas under trees, but it is risky to use them among the

The horned violet, *Viola cornuta*, makes an effective underplanting for old-fashioned roses, such as the Portland rose 'Comte de Chambord' seen here. The viola flowers over a long period throughout the summer, and seeds itself to fill any areas of bare soil.

more delicate shrubs as they can become invasive and difficult to remove without disturbing the roots of the plants they surround.

Bulbs and corms make more ephemeral ground cover, but they can look wonderful in their season. *Cyclamen hederifolium* has a double performance, with a solo show of flowers in autumn, followed by patterned leaves in winter and spring.

One way to enhance the performance of any plant is to place it in association with others that have complementary virtues. For instance, the lilac colour of *Viola cornuta* harmonizes especially well with the pinks and mauves of old roses. And planting old-fashioned pinks under roses gives a rich cocktail of scents as well as a subtle harmony of colour. Underplanting provides many opportunities for such associations. One of the highest achievements in the art of gardening is to plant a graduated border where the tallest plants, usually towards the back, are underplanted with slightly smaller plants, and so on towards the front, with each plant assisting to increase the impact of its neighbour. This art is perhaps at its most refined when the plants are selected to perform simultaneously in one single, harmonious chord. But it is equally valid when the arrangement is designed to extend the season, with the different plants reaching their peaks at different times.

Spring harmonies. The pink weeping cherry, *Prunus pendula* 'Pendula Rosea', is effectively underplanted with a mass of Dutch crocus in a range of colours from purple through lilac to white.

Making foliage flower

Another way to plant for all seasons, and to make
the best use of limited space, is to mask one plant's
weaknesses by putting it beside another with corresponding strengths. A perennial with striking
flowers but dull leaves, for example, can be grown
among foliage plants with modest flowers. The effect
is of a single plant of double value. Hostas, for instance, are among the best of the foliage plants, but
their striking flower spikes appear after the leaves
have begun to look rather tired. You can achieve a
virtuoso display in spring by interplanting hostas
with clumps of tulip bulbs to give the illusion
that the flowers are coming from the fresh green
leaves of the hostas. Foxgloves interplanted with
hostas or ferns give a similar effect later in the season. If you are really clever, you can achieve a progression of tulips first, then foxgloves, then the hosta

ABOVE The orange flowers
of *Crocosmia masoniorum*
seem to suit *Hosta fortunei
aureomarginata* better than
its own lilac flowers.

LEFT Yellow lily-flowered
tulips, planted among
hostas, create the illusion
that flowers and foliage
belong to the same plant.

RIGHT The flame creeper,
Tropaeolum speciosum, lights
up the dark foliage of a
topiary yew dome.

Clematis 'Rouge Cardinal'
in *Rosa glauca*

A Viticella clematis,
'Venosa Violacea', in
Cornus alba 'Elegantissima'

flowers themselves – all appearing to emerge from the same clumps of foliage.

Many shrubs and trees grown for their spring or autumn value can look dull at the height of summer. The flowering cherries, for instance, and the crab apples, may seem not to justify their space in the garden at the very time that the borders are at their glorious best. Growing climbing plants into such trees and shrubs cheats the passing of the months and brings interest to an otherwise dreary corner of the garden.

One group of flowering climbers is supreme above all others for adding a dash of colour to a tree or shrub in its drabbest season of the year. This is, of course, clematis. There are different clematis available to flower in every month. And they come in an astonishing range of colours, shapes and sizes. There are modest ground-hugging species that are best suited to the alpine trough or rockery. Others are so vigorous that they will cover the walls of a house within a few seasons. Clearly it is important to match your choice of clematis to the size and vigour of the host plant through which you plan to grow it. And the art of using clematis in this way is to match the flower with the foliage that it accompanies so that the two bring out the best in each other. The cleverest association of clematis that I have seen is the hybrid *C.* 'Rouge Cardinal' growing into the grey-leaved shrub *Rosa glauca*. This is a rose with modest flowers, but the clematis provides the flowers that the rose *ought* to have, of a colour that perfectly echoes the pink-flushed foliage.

RIGHT Another purple-leaved shrub, *Prunus cerasifera* 'Pissardii', is almost invisible under a curtain of the vigorous climber *Clematis* 'Perle d'Azur'. Lavender and fuchsia fill the gap below the shrub, with a variegated apple mint adding sparkle and a touch of scent. Although it may appear that the clematis has swamped its host shrub, it is very unlikely that a clematis of this type will do any damage. *Clematis montana* could be a different matter, as it makes such a tangle of growth that it can cut out the light to its host.

LEFT A strong contrast. The white *Clematis* 'Miss Bateman' shines out brightly from its host plant, the dwarf maple *Acer palmatum* 'Dissectum Atropurpureum'. A clever feature of this planting is that the purple-brown stamens of the clematis match the colour of the shrub's foliage.

The ornamental cabbage has earned a place in the flower border, where it offers colour and form over a long season. Here, in an autumn border, its purple tint combines well with Michaelmas daisies and annuals cosmos and echium. The annuals will be felled by the first hint of winter frosts, but the colour of the cabbage will only intensify with colder weather. Ornamental cabbages can be used just as effectively in more formal arrangements. At the celebrated garden of the château of Villandry in France, cabbages are planted in formal rows so that they entirely fill shaped beds enclosed by low box hedging. In this way they provide striking blocks that give the effect, at a distance, of a single colour.

Ornamental herbs, fruits and vegetables

Traditionally, fruits and vegetables have been relegated to a separate area, and, just as the kitchen was below stairs in the big house, so the kitchen garden was sometimes considered less important than the ornamental garden. Recently, however, more gardeners have discovered the ornamental value of herbs, fruits and vegetables, often as a result of visits to the great *potagers* in gardens such as Villandry, in Touraine, and Barnsley House, in Gloucestershire. One of the attractions of the formal *potager* is the arrangement of plants in straight rows. Another feature is the construction of interesting supports for climbing fruits and vegetables – patterned arrangements of canes for beans, and trellis and pergolas for vines, gourds and marrows. But even when they are taken out of this formal structure, many vegetables are attractive plants in their own right. The ornamental cabbage, for instance, well deserves a place in the flower border.

Some of the common fruit trees are exemplary plants for all seasons. An apple tree in blossom is one of the loveliest sights in springtime, and it performs again with a display of fruits that epitomizes autumn. It would surely be grown as an ornamental tree even if the fruits were inedible. The decorative value of fruit trees can be enhanced by the shapes into which they are trained. Parallel rows of apples may be arched to make a tunnel. Trained as espaliers, apples and pears make effective divisions between one garden 'room' and another. Espalier pears are suitable for growing against the walls of a house, where they make a feature that is every bit as attractive as the more conventional wisteria or Virginia creeper. You can extend the performance of apples and pears – as of other trees – by growing climbers into their branches, so that they are colourful with clematis or sweet peas even at times when their own displays are subdued.

Performing throughout the seasons

The pages that follow include a personal selection of plants that earn their place in the garden by the contribution they make throughout the year. You may find that some of your favourites are absent. Everybody loves old-fashioned roses, for instance, and no garden, however small, would be complete without them, even though the majority flower only once in the year. A splash of spring colour from tulips and narcissi is compulsory too. But these are not what I would call all-season plants. They are more like prima donnas that take centre stage for a spectacular but brief turn. Plants that perform over more than one season may be less ostentatious in their virtues, but a group of them will ensure a lasting display in the garden. Moreover – and this is the greatest test – you can arrange them so that they work together in · harmony, each one providing virtues complementary to those of its neighbours.

A pair of apple trees, trained on frameworks into goblet shapes in the *potager* of Barnsley House in Gloucestershire. Four main branches radiating from the stem have been trained vertically, with side-shoots aligned horizontally to create a dense structure on which the blossoms, and ultimately the fruits, are closely spaced. The main branches are arched over to give a rounded top to these decorative trees.

TIMELESS TREES

Trees are essential in any garden, for raising foliage above ground level to give a vertical element to the plant composition. Even the tiniest garden needs its complement of trees. They can even be grown in pots if necessary – it is surprising how well small trees will thrive in pots, provided that they are watered regularly.

The trees recommended here have been selected for features that they offer in addition to spring and summer foliage. Some have sensational blossom. Others have richly tinted leaves or colourful fruits in autumn. Winter is the time when you come to appreciate not only the enduring contribution of the evergreens, but also the bare outlines of the deciduous trees. Where a tree's silhouette is enhanced by brilliant bark colour, so much the better.

Trees are a sacred part of the landscape. Most gardeners love trees and will vigorously try to conserve them. This urge for conservation is right for the wild forests but it is not always appropriate in our gardens. So many gardens are ruined by trees that have grown too big for them. In my own garden it took me a year of vacillation before I could bring myself to remove an old yew tree which shaded the whole site and made gardening impossible. In the smallest gardens it may be necessary to replace trees quite often if it is not possible to keep them trimmed to size.

Gardening always involves a certain amount of artifice. Most plants, including trees, are amenable to a degree of manipulation. Topiary is the most extreme form, suitable for only a few trees, particularly yew. But many trees can be bent into shape to form arches or tunnels, trained as fans or espaliers against walls, or simply pruned to make mopheads. There are gardeners who regard such devices as an insult to nature. But if we wished to leave nature alone, we would not choose to make gardens.

A mature tree in its prime, this superb specimen of the dogwood *Cornus controversa* 'Variegata' is about twenty-five years old. Its early summer display of creamy-white flowers coincides with the successful underplanting of *Gladiolus communis* ssp. *byzantinus*. Like many of the dogwoods, this cornus has reddish young branches and twigs which give added interest after the autumn leaf fall.

Acer griseum in winter

Acer griseum

PAPER-BARK MAPLE
Peeling red bark, good autumn foliage

The maples are grown primarily for their brilliant autumn foliage and this goes for the paper-bark maple too. But this tree has the additional virtue of spectacular bark, which ensures that it remains interesting the whole year round. The bark of *Acer griseum* is quite unlike that of any other maple. Curling strips of the cinnamon-red outer bark peel off to expose the slightly less highly coloured young bark beneath. The bark peels continuously throughout the year, making the tree look rather like a red snake casting its skin.

Even without its special bark this tree would be worth growing for its foliage. The leaves are in three segments, with undulating margins. In spring the young leaves are a fresh pale green and they darken up as they mature. In autumn they colour to shades of fiery red.

The flowers and fruits of the acers are modest but attractive none the less. Loose panicles of reddish flowers hang down below the leaves in spring. They soon give rise to the double-winged seeds, commonly known as keys, which spin down in the wind when they mature.

● Height to 9m/30ft, spread to 7.5m/25ft. Full sun. Tolerant of any soil, but needs neutral to acid soil for good autumn colour. Zone 6

OTHER ACERS TO GROW

***Acer palmatum* 'Osakazuki'** This is one of the Japanese maples, and probably the best for autumn colour. Its broad leaves, with up to seven pointed lobes, take on a vivid hue of pure red in autumn, especially in neutral to acid soil. Height and spread to 4.5m/15ft. Zone 6

***Acer palmatum* 'Senkaki'** The coral-bark maple is another acer (also Japanese) with the double virtues of interesting bark and attractive foliage. The youngest twigs are a bright pinky red, which gives a stunning effect in winter. In autumn the leaves turn to amber-yellow, which looks especially good with the red stems showing through. Again, neutral to acid soil is needed for good autumn colour. Height and spread to 6m/20ft. Zone 6

Acer pensylvanicum A snakebark maple, with vertical stripes on the green bark that give the appearance of snakeskin. The bright green three-lobed leaves turn yellow in autumn. Height 6m/20ft,

Acer palmatum 'Osakazuki' in autumn

Acer palmatum 'Senkaki' in winter

spread 3.5m/12ft. Other good snakebark maples are *A. davidii* and *A. grosseri*, which grow to a height of 12m/40ft and a spread of 7.5m/25ft. Zone 4

***Acer platanoides* 'Drummondii'** This variety of the Norway maple has mid-green leaves edged with white. From a distance they give a bright shimmering effect. Height to 15m/50ft, spread 10.5m/35ft. Zone 3

***Acer pseudoplatanus* 'Brilliantissimum'** A sycamore with shrimp-pink young growth in spring turning through lime-green to green in summer. Height and spread to 6m/20ft. Any soil, full sun. Zone 6

Acer pensylvanicum in autumn

Acer griseum in autumn

Amelanchier lamarckii
in spring

Amelanchier lamarckii

SNOWY MESPILUS

Abundant white spring blossom, brilliant red and
orange autumn foliage

The quality of the blossom of any tree is decided as much as the presence or absence of leaves as by the flowers themselves. In the case of *Amelanchier lamarckii* the blossom coincides with the first growth of the young leaf shoots. These are the colour of worn copper and they impart metallic warmth to the clouds of slender white flowers that cover the tree.

The spring blossom is followed in autumn by small black berries, but these are of little ornamental value compared with the brilliance of the foliage, which erupts into shades of bright red and orange.

● Height to 6m/20ft, spread 4.5m/15ft. Sun or part-shade. Amelanchiers prefer a lime-free soil which, for the best autumn colour, should be on the acid side of neutral. According to the pruning regime, amelanchier may be grown either as a shrub or as a standard tree. Zone 4

OTHER AMELANCHIERS TO GROW

Amelanchier canadensis and **A. laevis** are also good amelanchiers, with attractive blossom and wonderful autumn colour. The different amelanchiers can be difficult to tell apart; they are all highly desirable. Zone 4

Betula utilis jacquemontii

WEST HIMALAYAN BIRCH

Pure white bark, catkins in spring, yellow autumn foliage

The birches are among the most graceful of trees. There are many striking species in the genus but *Betula utilis* var. *jacquemontii* is outstanding by virtue of its smooth and intensely white bark. This ensures that it is conspicuous in every season, but especially in winter. Then its whole framework is bare of leaves and it stands out like a sparkling white skeleton that has been picked clean by birds.

In common with all the birches, *B.u.* var. *jacquemontii* makes a graceful overall shape. It has delicate pointed oval leaves with serrated edges. These colour attractively to yellow in autumn, but the effect is very short-lived and for this reason the birches cannot be included among the most reliable trees for autumn colour. Their spring show, however, is more enduring, with the appearance of small catkins coinciding with the swelling and bursting open of the leaf buds.

• Height to 9m/30ft, spread 6m/20ft. Any soil. Tolerant of dry conditions. Although this birch makes a magnificent specimen tree, why not also consider planting several together in clumps? An odd number, say three or five trees, makes a natural-looking asymmetrical clump that might reasonably be considered three to five times more attractive than a single tree. Zone 6

OTHER BIRCHES TO GROW

Betula albosinensis A birch with pinky-white stems. Height 9m/30ft, spread 6m/20ft. Zone 6

Betula pendula 'Laciniata' (syn. 'Crispa') Sometimes wrongly called *B.p.* 'Dalecarlica'. An attractive form of the weeping birch, with finely cut leaves that enhance the drooping effect of the branches. Height 15m/50ft, spread 9m/30ft. Zone 2

Betula pendula 'Youngii' An elegant weeping birch. Its branches make an arching dome over a stem of white, marked with vertical black cracks. Height only to 7.5m/25ft and spread to 9m/30ft at maturity. Zone 2

Betula albosinensis catkins in spring

Betula utilis var. *jacquemontii* bark in winter

An autumn view of the *Cornus controversa* 'Variegata' that appears on page 22. The cream-variegated leaves have assumed a pinkish tinge. Soon they will fall and expose the red-barked younger branches which define the outlines of the distinctive tiered structure.

Cornus controversa 'Variegata'

Variegated leaves, dramatic summer flower display, red stems revealed in autumn and winter

One of the most elegant trees available, *Cornus controversa* 'Variegata' has broadly sweeping horizontal branches that grow in tiers, tapering from a wide base near the ground to a point at the apex. The pyramidal shape alone would be enough to make this cornus a very special tree, but it has the additional attraction of cream-variegated leaves.

Furthermore, in summer the tiered branches are covered with a froth of white flowers, like creamy confections on a tablecloth. In autumn the leaves turn slightly pink before dropping to reveal the red twigs that are characteristic of many of the dogwoods. The only thing that can be said against this marvellous tree is that it is extremely slow-growing.

With its horizontal thrust and bright foliage *C.c.* 'Variegata' looks especially good against a background of upright conifers which supply a contrast of both tone and shape.

Cornus kousa var. *chinensis* in summer

Cornus kousa var. *chinensis* in autumn

Cornus mas flowers in winter

• This cornus eventually becomes a stately specimen 9m/30ft in height and spread. Does best in full sun and well-drained fertile soil, preferably neutral to acid. Zone 6

OTHER CORNUS TO GROW

Cornus florida An attractive tree, with white or pinkish-white flower bracts and leaves that turn red in autumn. There are several forms available, including *C. florida* f. *rubra*, which has flat mid-pink bracts. All do best in slightly acid soils. Height to 5.5m/18ft, spread 6m/20ft. Zone 6

Cornus kousa var. chinensis This tree in full flower in summer is a sensation. The branches are so densely crowded with pure white flower bracts that the leaves become almost invisible – the effect is of broad white clouds filling the garden with light. The tree puts on a second performance in autumn when the foliage colours up brilliantly and the flowers develop into hanging red fruits. The leaves are mid-green, turning to a flaming red before they fall. Height to 6m/20ft, spread to 4.5m/15ft. Zone 5

Cornus mas The cornelian cherry is an unostentatious tree, but attractive as one of the first harbingers of spring. It is covered with a haze of fragrant tiny yellow flowers on bare twigs while winter snows may still be on the ground. These give rise later to edible red fruits that look like cherries but do not taste so well. Height and spread to 6m/20ft. Zone 5

This beech hedge, here assuming its autumn tints, makes a substantial boundary to a small enclosure within a much larger garden. When the hedge was planted, a space was left for a path to cross; as the adjacent trees grew, branches were trained across, tied together and pruned to make an arch. The beauty of a beech hedge is that it retains its leaves for most of the year – fresh lime-green in spring and brown in winter.

Fagus sylvatica

COMMON BEECH

Soft lime-green young foliage, brown autumn leaves remaining over winter

It is a curious phenomenon that the stately beech tree loses its leaves soon after they have coloured up in autumn, whereas the same plant, clipped and grown as a hedge, keeps its leaves throughout the winter. The beech tree becomes a winter skeleton but the beech hedge retains its splendid autumn colour of sienna brown until the dead leaves are finally pushed off by new growth in spring. This retention of leaves is said to be a juvenile characteristic, but it can be induced in older trees by constant pruning.

Next to yew and box, beech is perhaps the most useful hedging available for creating screens and divisions and allées within the garden. Because of the relatively large size of its leaves, it is not suitable for low hedges, which would be better made from box, *Buxus sempervirens*.

● To plant your hedge, place the young trees about 30cm/12in apart in a trench prepared with plenty of manure. Trim in autumn, from the outset, to encourage bushy growth. Zone 5

ANOTHER BEECH TO GROW

Fagus sylvatica purpurea The copper beech is the favourite of many gardeners as a specimen tree, and it can equally well be the choice for a magnificent copper-coloured hedge. It is even more effective to mix the two forms at random to produce a tapestry of overlapping colours. Zone 5

Liriodendron tulipifera

TULIP TREE

Unusual leaves, colouring well in autumn; on mature trees, bell-shaped flowers in summer

Liriodendron tulipifera
flower in summer

You will need plenty of space and a thought for the next generation if your tulip tree is to fulfil its maximum potential. This stately tree eventually reaches a height of 30m/100ft, and it will not flower until it is at least 7.5m/25ft high and around fifteen years old. So perhaps it is irresponsible of me to suggest that you could consider planting a tulip tree in even the smallest garden: it might be too frustrating to have to take it out before it reached more than a small fraction of its final size. But I have seen a tulip tree grown in a pot on a roof garden to great effect – grown entirely for its lovely foliage.

The tulip tree's leaves are unlike those of any other tree, unless you can picture a maple leaf with its pointed tip cut off square like a flour scoop. They are mid-green and smooth to the touch and in autumn they colour to a glorious butter-yellow. It would be striking to underplant the tree with a mass of the autumn-flowering bulb *Colchicum speciosum*, which has large, crocus-like, pale magenta flowers.

The tree, of course, is named for its flowers, which have only a passing resemblance to tulips. They are shaped like upright bells, the tips of the petals curling over slightly to form a lip. The flower is in an unusual combination of colours. The ribbon-shaped stamens which fill the centre of the bell are pale orange, and the ground colour of the petals is a greeny cream, but they are marked from the base with a spreading stain of orange. The flowers are about 6cm/2½in across, quite small in relation to the size of the mature tree on which they appear.

• Height to 30m/100ft, spread 15m/50ft. Prefers fertile, well-drained and slightly acid soil. Propagate by seed. Zone 5

Liriodendron tulipifera 'Aureomarginatum'

OTHER LIRIODENDRONS TO GROW

Liriodendron tulipifera 'Aureomarginatum' In this superb variegated variety the leaves are edged with a variable band of yellow. The overall effect of the tree is a shimmering golden haze, and it will give intense pleasure even as a small tree. Could be grown in a tub. Zone 5

Liriodendron tulipifera 'Fastigiatum' If you only have a medium-sized garden but are determined to grow a tulip tree to flowering size, then you should obtain this narrow-growing form, which attains the same height as the standard tree but takes up less lateral space. Zone 5

Trained as espaliers, dessert eating apples make an effective boundary hedge. Spring and autumn are obviously the peak seasons for display, but even in winter the trained trees, bare of leaf, have a strikingly graphic structure, like a living fence. Apples and pears can also be trained to make a tunnel over a path. This involves training cordon trees over arched metal supports. Structures like this need constant maintenance — they can easily get out of hand if growth is allowed to go unchecked. But it is very rewarding to pick fruit from a hedge or tunnel that is part of the formal structure of your garden. If the idea takes your fancy you can have further fun by pruning bush fruits such as gooseberries and redcurrants into standards or fans, and by training vegetables like marrows and gourds into arches.

Malus domestica

EATING APPLE

Spring blossom, autumn fruits, amenable to ornamental training

There are few sights more lovely in the garden than an apple tree in full bloom, with the first bees of the spring excitedly working their way through the prodigality of blossom. Again in the autumn, the apple becomes the symbol of its season, weighed down with fruits of green and golden red. Yet such is the culinary value of the apple that its usefulness as an ornamental tree is sometimes overlooked.

Over the centuries growers have selected a phenomenally wide range of apple varieties, according to the flavour, texture and colour of the fruit and to their season of flowering and fruiting. The grafting, pruning and shaping of apples has been elevated to the level of a fine art. All this accumulated wisdom about apples can be intimidating, but growing apples is simple, provided you bear three things in mind. First, you need to be aware of rootstocks. These are graded according to their vigour. If you wish to grow apples decoratively, as fans and espaliers, you must buy plants with a dwarfing rootstock, or else your trees will be too vigorous to control. The most commonly used rootstock for this purpose is M26. For cordons you need even less vigour: go for M9 rootstock. If you have room for only tiny bushes in your garden, choose the most dwarfing rootstock of all, M27.

Second, apples are not self-pollinating. This means that if you grow a single apple tree in isolation, out of bee-range of any other apple, the flowers will not be fertilized, and you will have no fruit. So, unless neighbouring gardens are well endowed with apple trees, it is best to grow two or more together: if necessary they can be kept small, by choosing an appropriate rootstock and by pruning. Choose varieties that come into blossom at the same time –

there can be a gap of several weeks between different groups. The ornamental crab apples will function as pollinators and they are sometimes grown in commercial orchards for this purpose.

The third choice that you face is the more personal one of fruit type. Do you want cooking apples or eaters? Early or late fruiting? You will, of course, have your own preferences for flavour, but you might also think about colour – green, yellow or red apples? If you have room for a selection, you could consider some of the varieties listed in the table below.

A well-trained apple fan or espalier is a lovely thing. Trained against a wall or fence a tree will take up minimum space but will produce a bounty of flowers and fruits. Even more effective, to my mind, are free-standing fans and espaliers, trained along wires strung between posts. Planted in rows, these can make the most attractive garden-dividers – open

Malus 'Cox's Orange Pippin'

Malus 'Ingrid Marie'

Variety (type)	Fruit colour	Flower season	Fruit season
Beauty of Bath (dessert)	red and yellow	early	very early
Discovery (dessert)	red and green	early	very early
James Grieve (dessert)	green	mid	early
Worcester Pearmain (dessert)	red and green	mid	early
Egremont Russet (dessert)	khaki	early	mid
Ingrid Marie (dessert)	deep red	late	mid
Lord Lambourne (dessert)	red and yellow	early	mid
Cox's Orange Pippin (dessert)	red and green	mid	late
Laxton's Superb (dessert)	red and green	late	very late
Grenadier (cooking)	yellow	mid	early
Bramley's Seedling (cooking)	green	mid	late
Howgate Wonder (cooking)	red and green	mid	late

enough to allow glimpses through, but sufficiently dense to form a simple enclosure-hedge. Delightful from both sides in blossom and again in fruit, these look striking in winter too, when their filigree architecture becomes the main attraction.

Another way to create an apple hedge is to use cordons – individual plants pruned to a single stem with short side-shoots along its length. You can use cordons trained parallel at a slant, at 90cm/36in intervals, but this can look a little regimental. It is more effective to train alternate cordons in opposite directions, so that they create a living trellis structure. This way, you might choose to construct an apple tunnel with cordon lattices on each side of a path and further cordons at regular intervals trained around an arch to meet overhead. You can manipulate a free-standing bush too, to give it the shape you want: for example, by arching the branches upwards and inwards by tying them to a framework, you create a compact and elegant goblet-shaped bush. You might favour a flat-bottomed cone-shaped tree, which is created by anchoring the tips of the lowest branches to the ground, so that they grow out horizontally to the stem, and then trimming the upper branches to shape.

With one exception, there are no short cuts to all these special effects in fruit trees and a strict pruning routine must be followed from the start. The exception is the new Ballerina apple, which is like a naturally growing cordon, requiring no pruning to preserve its columnar shape. This makes it especially useful for the small low-maintenance garden. However, to make the most of the apple's possibilities, there is no substitute for string, secateurs and sweat.

• Height and spread to 9m/30ft, but dimensions can be controlled by choice of rootstock and by pruning. Any soil. Benefits from an annual topdressing of manure. A winter spray of tar wash will keep many of the undesirable bugs at bay. Zone 3

LEFT In a tiny front garden that runs beside a terrace of cottages, the only place to grow fruit is against the wall. Here an ancient espalier pear gives a generous eiderdown of blossom. This will be followed by an autumn crop that should keep the household in fruit for several weeks.

RIGHT A ring of young crab apples creates a small garden enclosure. Trained as fans and espaliers, the trees will make an informal hedge with dual seasons of interest. Here the rose-pink blossoms of *Malus* 'Profusion' complement the pink tulips beyond. The white-flowered *Malus* 'Golden Hornet' will produce a spectacular display of small yellow apples in autumn.

OTHER FRUIT TREES TO GROW
ORNAMENTALLY

Pears are as amenable as apples to pruning and training to decorative shapes. As with apples, two plants are required for pollination.

Plums and cherries are suitable for training into ornamental fans. Many plums, including the popular 'Victoria', are self-fertile. The cooking cherry, the 'Morello', is self-fertile and may also be used as a pollinator of sweet cherries. Among the sweet cherries themselves there is one variety, 'Stella', that is self-fertile.

Malus 'Golden Hornet'

GOLDEN CRAB APPLE
Prolific spring blossom, autumn fruits
that last into winter

Some of the crab apples, like their cousins the domestic apples, are star performers that put on a double act of equal value in spring and autumn. They are also reliable and easy to grow. They are small trees that will not get out of hand, and if you need to restrict their growth for a very small garden, they can be kept compact by pruning. There is a wide choice of varieties that have been selected for their blossom,

Spring and autumn effects. Crab apples and flowering cherries alternate in this avenue that leads to a pretty stone summerhouse. The two crab apples in the foreground are *Malus* 'Golden Hornet'.

and colour and size of fruit. Among the best is *Malus* 'Golden Hornet'.

In spring, 'Golden Hornet' is covered with clusters of clear white flowers, about 2.5cm/1in across, along the length of its branches. The only quibble that you might have about this spring display is that it is not very long-lasting – a week or so at the most. The fragile blossom is easily scattered by a strong wind. The autumn fruits more than compensate for the short life of the blossom – they survive on the tree for several months, well into winter and long

after the leaves have been shed. These fruits are miniature apples, about 2.5cm/1in long, golden yellow in colour and hanging in bunches along the branches. Crab apples are bitter-tasting, but they can be cooked to make a delicious jelly. However, though using windfalls for cooking is permissible, picking crab apples is sacrilege in my book. The whole point of growing the tree is for ornament. In a good season a mature tree will be weighed down under its burden of fruits, glowing golden in the autumn sun.

Unlike some of the domestic apples, crabs like 'Golden Hornet' are self-fertile. This means that a single tree will produce fruit. However, it is said that fertilization is improved if several crabs are grown together, and, provided you have the space, this is in any case an effective way to use them. The crabs are usually grown as standard trees but there is no reason why they should not be pruned to make fans, espaliers or goblets, just like domestic apples (see pages 33-4). I admit that I have never seen this done, but I cannot think why not. I have started to train two 'Golden Hornets' as espaliers in my own garden, but it is still too early to report on the results.

It is a test for a gardener to provide effective associations for trees like these that perform in two seasons. Of course the spring display coincides with the peak season for bulbs, and a carpet of cream or white flowering bulbs makes a stunning underplanting to *M.* 'Golden Hornet'. You might try *Narcissus* 'Thalia', with its multi-headed white flowers, or cream *N.* 'Mount Hood' and the white *Tulipa* 'Purissima' – but you will need to be very clever, or

Malus 'Golden Hornet' blossom

Malus 'Golden Hornet' fruits

Malus 'Red Sentinel' fruits

Malus 'Evereste' fruits

very lucky, for their flowering to coincide precisely with that of the crab. These bulbs can be interplanted with shrubs chosen to combine with the second performance of the tree. Here you might pick plants with fiery autumn colours, such as cotinus, fothergilla or deciduous azaleas, though some of these will thrive only on an acid soil. Among these autumn treasures the yellow crab apples will shine like amber jewels.

- Height to 6m/20ft, spread to 4.5m/15ft. Any well-drained soil, in sun or part-shade. *M.* 'Golden Hornet' will benefit from an annual top-dressing of well-rotted manure. If necessary, prune to keep compact; otherwise, just cut out any dead wood and trim to keep the canopy in good shape. Zone 5

OTHER CRAB APPLES TO GROW

Malus floribunda The Japanese crab is probably the loveliest in flower, with dark pink buds opening to pale pink flowers which completely cover the tree. Height and spread to 4.5m/15ft. Zone 5

Malus hupehensis The mature tree is larger than the average crab. The white flowers, pink in bud, are large too, up to 3cm/1½in across, and fragrant. Small red fruits. For good orange-red fruits try *Malus* 'Red Sentinel' and for scarlet fruits *Malus* 'Evereste'. Height to 9m/30ft, spread to 6m/20ft. Zone 5

***Malus* 'Profusion'** A more upright variety, with purple leaves in spring, maturing to dark green. The flowers have a deep rose tint, and the tiny fruits are red. Height to 6m/20ft, spread to 3.5m/12ft. Zone 5

Malus sargentii A dwarf species, suitable for the smallest garden. The leaves are unusual, with three lobes. Small white flowers are followed by tiny red fruits. Height and spread to 2.5m/8ft. Zone 5

Ostrya virginiana fruits

Ostrya virginiana

HOP HORNBEAM OR IRONWOOD
Spring catkins, hop-like fruits in autumn

A deciduous tree from the eastern United States, the hop hornbeam is an asset in the garden throughout the year, but it has two special seasons of glory. In spring the branches are hung with the delicate tassels of the male catkins. These are green-yellow and appear before the hornbeam-like leaves open, making a striking sight when seen against the spring sky. In autumn the curious leafy fruits hang from the tree. They look like hops and they are greeny white when they first appear. They turn brown later, as the tree's foliage turns to gold.

• Height to 15m/50ft, spread 12m/40ft. Any soil. Zone 5

Ostrya virginiana catkins

LEFT TO RIGHT *Prunus × subhirtella* 'Autumnalis' in autumn, in early winter, in midwinter and in spring

Prunus × subhirtella 'Autumnalis'

AUTUMN-FLOWERING CHERRY

Pinkish-white flowers throughout the winter, autumn foliage colour

Any tree that blossoms all through the winter is a boon in the garden; one that also provides autumn colour is a double treasure. For a week or two in mid-autumn, the leaves of *Prunus × subhirtella* 'Autumnalis' turn a brilliant hue of rusty orange. The flower buds are already swelling, and by the time the last leaves have fallen, the first of the pinkish-white flowers have opened. If the weather is mild, the tree will soon be covered with blossom, giving the happy illusion that winter has passed by unnoticed and spring is already here.

I have seen the blossom of this tree covered with a rime of frost and surviving, but a spell of cold weather depresses further flowering for a time. However, this prunus will go on giving a few flowers throughout the winter, especially in warm spells. Bare branches picked in midwinter can usually be coaxed into flower in a vase beside the fire. Then, in early spring, after almost six months of intermittent activity, the tree will often have a final burst of flower as the leaves begin to open.

During the summer this tree, like many flowering cherries, looks relatively undistinguished. Be sure to buy a shapely specimen at the start – its shape is all it has to offer when the rest of your garden is at its peak. One way to get it to contribute to the garden's summer activity is to grow a climber through it. Choose a vigorous clematis, like Viticella clematis 'Abundance', as the tree has a dense canopy. Plant it at least 1.2m/4ft away from the trunk, as the prunus has dense and shallow roots, and provide a cane for the clematis to climb up into the tree.

The tree is suitable for the smallest garden, and should flower in the first season that you buy it. The equally attractive variety *P.* × *s.* 'Autumnalis Rosea' has pink flowers.

If I had room for only one tree in the garden, this would be it. The gift of spring in winter is as precious as a whole bed of summer flowers.

● Height and spread to 6m/20ft. Prefers full sun. All prunus species are rather shallow-rooted and this can be detrimental to shrubs and other plants growing nearby. *Prunus* × *subhirtella* 'Autumnalis' is usually grafted on to the rootstock of another species: check that the graft is near ground level, as this produces the best-shaped tree. Zone 6

A line of *Prunus serrula* brings colour into the garden in winter as well as summer. This summer view shows *Echinops bannaticus* in the foreground, and behind it the purple foliage of another useful cherry, *Prunus cerasifera* 'Pissardii', planted as a hedge at the back of the border.

OTHER PRUNUS TO GROW

***Prunus cerasifera* 'Pissardii'** The purple-leaved plum is covered in small white blossoms in early spring. The red-purple leaves follow. Makes a good hedge. Height and spread to 9m/30ft. Zone 4

***Prunus pendula* 'Pendula Rosea'** (syn. *P. × sub-hirtella* 'Pendula') A weeping tree with spring flowers of a rich pink. Height and spread to 6m/20ft. Zone 6

Prunus serrula Modest in flower but treasured for its bark, which is shiny fox-red. This makes it one of the most striking trees in winter. Height and spread to 9m/30ft. Zone 6

Prunus 'Shōgetsu' (syn. *P. serrulata longipes*) One of the best of the Japanese cherries, making a broad spreading shape, covered with pure white flowers in spring. The leaves colour magnificently in autumn. Height to 6m/20ft, spread 7.5m/25ft. Zone 6

Salix alba 'Britzensis'

SCARLET WILLOW

Spring catkins, orange-brown stems for winter colour

The willows range from the stately weeping willow, familiar as a specimen tree in many large gardens, to tiny, prostrate forms that belong in the alpine garden. Many have fluffy catkins appearing before the foliage in spring. The varieties with coloured stems also look sensational in winter. Among the best of these is *Salix alba* 'Britzensis' (syn. 'Chermesina').

With this willow it is only the young stems that have bark of a fiery orange-brown colour: after the first year the old wood becomes relatively dull. So you have to be merciless with the secateurs each year to ensure plenty of young growth and to get the best decorative value from the plant. If grown as a shrub, this willow should be pruned on the coppicing principle by cutting right back to the woody framework at ground level in spring, just before the leaf buds open. Then it has the whole summer to put out twiggy new growth for next winter's display. If it is grown as a standard tree, the principle is the same except that pruning is done on the pollarding basis, by cutting back the young branches to within a few centimetres of the main trunk of the tree.

Unfortunately, with this plant you cannot have the best of both worlds. If it is pruned as vigorously as I propose for the maximum winter effect, you will miss out on the decorative spring catkins. The ideal solution, if you have space, is to grow several willows together, choosing some species for their colourful catkins, others primarily for their bark.

● Left to its own devices, *S.a.* 'Britzensis' will make a tree with a height of 25m/80ft and spread of 15m/50ft. However, coppiced annually as described, it can be kept to a rounded shrub with a height and spread of 1.8m/6ft. Full sun, any soil, but needs plenty of moisture for best results. Zone 2

OTHER WILLOWS TO GROW

All will flourish in any soil, provided they have sufficient moisture.

Salix alba* var. *vitellina The golden willow has butter-yellow stems that stand out prominently in winter, especially against a dark background. For best stem effect, prune vigorously in spring, as above. Unpruned, it will make an attractive tree, growing to about 15m/50ft. Zone 2

***Salix caprea* 'Kilmarnock'** A compact tree for a small garden, the weeping pussy willow produces curtains of branches from a central trunk, arching down to ground level. In spring these are covered

ABOVE *Salix gracilistyla* 'Melanostachys' is grown primarily for its spring catkins.

LEFT *Salix alba* 'Britzensis' in late autumn. Pruned regularly to give colourful young stems, this willow makes a graceful and compact shrub.

with powder-puff catkins with bright yellow anthers which are a favourite destination for early flights of bees. For a good overall effect, underplant with spring flowers that will not mind being shaded when the tree is later covered with leaves – narcissi or polyanthus primroses, for example. Height and spread 1.8m/6ft. Zone 5

Salix daphnoides The violet willow has purple shoots, overlaid with a white bloom which gives them a misty violet colour. For the best stem effects hard pruning is necessary. Zone 5

Salix gracilistyla One of the best shrubs for catkins. The immature male catkins are silvery grey and silky in texture, opening into an upright, elongated shape with bright yellow anthers. Height 3m/10ft, spread 3.5m/12ft. The variety 'Melanostachys' has very dark catkins, with yellow anthers. Zone 6

Salix lanata A dwarf species, up to 1.2m/4ft in height and spread, grown for its lovely grey foliage. The leaves are broad and woolly and they open in spring in the company of the yellow-anthered catkins. Suitable for the rock garden or beside a small pond. Zone 2

Salix × sepulcralis var. chrysocoma The weeping willow is seen at its best as a specimen plant with plenty of space around it, or growing beside a lake or river, where its long, pendulous branches will lap the water. Narrow, lance-shaped leaves are bright green in spring, yellow in autumn and mid-green between these seasons. It is a fabulous sight in midwinter with its long, hanging twigs a brilliant golden yellow. Needs sun and plenty of moisture in any soil. Height and spread to 18m/60ft. Zone 5

Salix caprea 'Kilmarnock' in spring

Sorbus aria 'Lutescens'

WHITEBEAM

White spring foliage, autumn fruit
and foliage colour

The whitebeam's maximum impact is in the spring, when the buds unfurl to give young leaves that are slightly woolly to the touch and silvery white to the eye. The tree seems to glow with this new growth and, for me at least, it is one of the most potent symbols of spring.

There are several forms of whitebeam and most of them lose their ethereal haze of white after the first flush of spring. *Sorbus aria* 'Lutescens' is the best variety because it retains at least a vestige of whiteness in the mature leaves. This quality comes from a white bloom, or 'tomentum', that covers the leaves, like the bloom on the skin of a newly picked plum.

The tree's white flowers, borne in late spring, tend to merge into the general whiteness of the foliage. The autumn fruits however, are conspicuous red berries, a vivid touch of pure colour against the brownish background of the turning leaves.

● Height to 12m/40ft, spread 7.5m/25ft. Any soil, including over chalk. Suitable for urban and seaside planting as it is tolerant of pollution and salty air. Zone 6

An unusual and effective arch of *Sorbus aria* 'Lutescens' at Kiftsgate Court in Gloucestershire. The arch was created by planting young trees at each side and training them on to a metal support. Regular trimming encourages dense and bushy growth.

Sorbus hupehensis 'Rosea' berries in autumn

floral department, as almost all of them flower in late spring with white flowers held in flat heads above the leaves. There is some diversity in foliage though. They all have ash-like leaves with many leaflets fanning out from a central midriff but some species have fine filigree leaflets and others have coarser foliage. In some species, but not all, the leaves give fiery autumn colours. There are erect varieties among them and there are weeping ones. But the main basis of choice is in the colour of the berries. According to your preference you can go for red berries or yellow, or for shades of orange in between. Or you might venture to the slightly less common species which have white or pink berries.

On balance, if I could choose only one, I believe

Sorbus hupehensis

HUBEI ROWAN

Spring flowers, delicate foliage that colours red in autumn, and white or pink fruits that last into winter

The rowans or mountain ashes are such a large and desirable group of trees that it is difficult to select any one as being especially preferable to the others: almost all of them are fine plants for all seasons, attractive in all their parts and at all times of the year. There is little to choose between them in the

Sorbus cashmiriana flowers in spring

that it would have to be a form of the rowan of Chinese origin, *Sorbus hupehensis*. In *S. hupehensis* itself the berries are white with just a hint of pink around their tips. The stalks that hold the berries are vivid scarlet, and the leaves provide a delicate grey-green tracery all around, so that from a distance the tree in early autumn has a pale and enchantingly ghostly appearance. Later in the season the leaves turn red.

The pink-berried variety, 'Rosea', is perhaps even more beautiful. As the berries begin to colour up in autumn to a warm peachskin pink, the grey-green leaves pick up a pinkish tinge as if in sympathy. Later the leaves turn reddish brown before falling, to leave the clusters of berries still hanging gracefully from the bare branches.

Sorbus cashmiriana berries in autumn

● Height eventually 15m/50ft and spread 7.5m/25ft, but it will take a long time to reach that scale. In a small garden it will give many years of pleasure before it grows too big for its site. Any well-drained soil. Zone 6

OTHER SORBUS TO GROW

Sorbus aucuparia In this, the European rowan, the leaflets have toothed edges like a saw and are relatively coarse. The foliage turns a golden orange in autumn, making a fiery combination with the vivid orange-red berries of the species. Height up to 10.5m/35ft, spread 7.5m/25ft. There is also a variety, *S. a.* 'Fructu Luteo' (syn. 'Xanthocarpa'), which has amber-yellow berries. Other rowans with red berries and good autumn foliage are *S. commixta* and its variety 'Embley'. Both have an erect habit with feathered branches. Zone 3

Sorbus cashmiriana A handsome rowan with bunches of white berries in autumn, accompanied by golden-brown leaves. Height to 9m/30ft, spread 7.5m/25ft. Another good choice for white berries is *S. prattii*. In a good autumn, it looks like a snowstorm. *S. cashmiriana* is hardy to zone 5, *S. prattii* to zone 3.

Sorbus 'Joseph Rock' A tree of upright habit with golden-yellow fruits which make a lovely combination with the autumn tints of its leaves. These turn through shades of orange, yellow and purplish green. Height to 10.5m/35ft, spread 6m/20ft. Zone 5

Sorbus vilmorinii One of the most petite-looking rowans, with very fine dark grey-green leaflets and gracefully arching branches. The leaves turn to bronze-red in autumn to accompany the loose clusters of pink berries. Height and spread to 4.5m/15ft. Zone 6

Sorbus commixta berries in autumn

Sorbus 'Joseph Rock' berries in autumn

Immaculate topiary in yew. The hedge has been clipped as flat as a table top but at regular intervals the leaders of some of the constituent plants have been allowed to grow upwards and shaped to make simplified mushrooms and birds.

Taxus baccata

COMMON YEW

A versatile evergreen for hedges and topiary

The common yew can be a lugubrious tree. Grown as a free-standing specimen it casts such dense shade that nothing will grow happily beneath it. Its evergreen foliage is such a dark green that it may appear black in comparison with its garden neighbours. This tree looks most at home in a graveyard, where its sombre presence lends an appropriately funereal air and its evergreen foliage can be taken as a symbol for everlasting life.

It may seem surprising to commend the yew, with its morbid associations, as a key plant to supply the background structure to any garden, however large or small. But it has a quality that makes it outstanding: its almost infinite capacity for regeneration. The more punishment it receives from trimming and shaping, the more densely it sprouts new

growth. This makes it one of the best plants for hedging or for topiary. A yew hedge makes a perfect boundary or partition within a garden. As a background to a border its sombre tone sets off the brighter plants. It can be effective too when shaped into buttresses to divide a border into compartments. Yew looks good as an arch over a gateway or as an isolated topiary shape, whether of a rigidly geometric form like a pyramid, cylinder or cone, or else as a more whimsical creation such as a dove or a peacock.

Because of the great age of some venerable yew trees, people tend to assume that yew is very slow-growing. This is not strictly true, and it is quite possible to establish a good yew hedge or a shapely piece of topiary within, say, eight years of putting in young plants. What is true, however, is that a yew structure can be 'frozen' in a desired shape, once it is established, by judicious pruning of new growth. Some topiary gardens have remained virtually unchanged for decades, with only an annual 'haircut' needed to keep them in shape.

If you follow my advice and restrict the yews in your garden to hedging and topiary, I admit that you will probably miss two rather attractive features of the plant. First the trunk, seen best in a mature tree, is full of character, bumpy and twisted and covered with scaly mahogany-red bark. And the fruits, borne most freely on an unpruned tree, are unexpected on a conifer and an attractive bonus. Ripening in autumn and persisting into winter, they are like oblong red buttons, of the consistency of jelly babies – but do not let your children or pets eat them. The single seed inside is highly poisonous.

• An unpruned mature yew tree will reach a height of 12m/40ft and a spread of 9m/30ft. As a hedge, yew can be maintained at a height of, say, 2.5m/8ft by regular trimming. In the wild, *T. baccata* grows on dry chalk soils. In cultivation too it thrives in alkaline conditions, but it is perfectly tolerant of acid soils, provided that there is good drainage. When planting a yew hedge, allow 60cm/24in between plants and give them a good start by mixing a generous handful of bonemeal with the earth around their roots. As with any plant, the rate of growth is dependent upon regular watering and feeding in the growing period. For hedging or topiary, trim the side-shoots in late summer to encourage bushy growth, but keep the main leader until it has reached the required height. When growing a yew hedge behind a border, it is a good idea to construct an underground barrier of corrugated iron or thick plastic to deflect the hedge roots from the border. Otherwise, a mature hedge can seriously deplete the soil of moisture and nutriments needed by the border plants. Zone 6

OTHER YEWS TO GROW

***Taxus baccata* 'Elegantissima'** The new growth of this yew is yellow, later fading to green. It is slower-growing than the common yew, but much less gloomy. Ideal if you are looking for a yellow hedging or topiary plant. Zone 6

***Taxus baccata* 'Fastigiata'** The Irish yew is a good architectural tree, with upward-pointing branches giving a tapering, columnar shape. It forms a slim column when young but in a mature tree – which may be up to 4.5m/15ft high – the branches tend to spread a little and may need to be tied in with hoops of string or wire. This tree is particularly useful if you want a formal effect combined with easy maintenance. Planted at regular intervals along a drive or allée, Irish yews make neat and repetitive columns – but with rough edges. Zone 6

***Taxus baccata* 'Standishii'** Another columnar form, even more tightly erect than the Irish yew, but very slow-growing. Golden-green foliage. Zone 6

Taxus baccata 'Fastigiata' berries

Taxus baccata 'Standishii'

DOUBLE-VALUE SHRUBS AND CLIMBERS

A garden is much more than a collection of plants. The way in which you group and associate your plants will determine the character of your garden, making it particular to you alone. Gone are the days when shrubs were to be grown in 'shrubberies', away from other plants. The modern garden tends to be a medley of trees, shrubs, perennials and annuals all mixed in together. Shrubs provide the foundations of the mixed border, because they form the largest and least mobile elements in it. Perennials and annuals can be juggled around each year with impunity, but shrubs make deeper roots and resent being moved.

Many shrubs, such as berberis, cornus and cotinus, are selected primarily for their foliage. Flowers, fruits or coloured stems come as a bonus. With the roses, the ultimate in flower power, the bonus comes in the form of hips, autumn foliage colour, or decorative thorns.

Most shrubs (like most trees) are amenable to pruning and training. You can make hedges by multiple plantings of box and berberis, for instance. More tender shrubs, like choisya, will often benefit from being trained against a wall. This gives them protection against cold and also provides a flat base against which they can produce a perfect foliage backcloth.

Climbers, generically, are the most useful of plants, not only for clothing walls and screening unsightly structures but also for associating with trees and shrubs. Plants that are in action in different seasons can be particularly effective when grown together. Growing climbers like clematis or wisteria through earlier-flowering shrubs or trees is one way to cheat the passing of the months.

A small town garden, superbly planted with a framework of shrubs, and decorated with swathes of climbers. The plants are graduated by height, with trees around the perimeter. These include a golden elm (top left), the yellow-leaved *Robinia pseudoacacia* 'Frisia' and the purple-leaved *Prunus cerasifera* 'Pissardii' (top right). Occupying the middle ground are conifers and shrubs including *Lonicera nitida* 'Baggesen's Gold' (with small yellow leaves) draped with purple-blue *Clematis × durandii*. Plants in the centre of the scheme include *Lavatera trimestris* 'Silver Cup', *Campanula persicifolia*, astilbes and (in the foreground) *Lychnis coronaria* 'Oculata'. In this masterpiece of planting the smallest plants, low-growing polygonums, grasses and pulmonaria, are grouped at the front alongside the path.

Aronia arbutifolia

RED CHOKEBERRY

White spring flowers, red leaves and berries in autumn

The aronia's period of glory is in autumn when its foliage turns a fiery red and matches the shiny red berries that mature at the same time. It is one of the better medium-sized shrubs for autumn colour, but it is not sufficiently distinguished for the rest of the year to stand on its own as a specimen shrub. It looks well in a mixed planting with other plants grown for their foliage, such as maples. Here it will contribute its own special flame to the general fire that sweeps the border in autumn. It would be a good neighbour to *Cotinus coggygria* 'Royal Purple', because the leaf shapes of the two shrubs make a pleasing contrast.

The aronia has a narrow, pointed leaf in comparison to the broad, rounded leaf of the cotinus. What is more, the two plants colour to different shades of red, the aronia to scarlet, the cotinus to a dusky velvet crimson.

The pretty little flowers of *Aronia arbutifolia* are typical of the rose family, to which the shrub belongs. About 2.5cm/1in across, they are white and single with five petals each, reminiscent of the blossom of an apple or crab apple tree but not usually so abundant.

● Height and spread to 2.5m/8ft. Sun or part-shade. Like many shrubs grown for autumn colour, aronias produce the best effects when grown on neutral to acid soils. Propagate by cuttings. Zone 5

Matching pictures of *Aronia arbutifolia* show its spring performance of a mass of small white flowers, rather like apple blossom, followed by vivid red foliage in autumn. The brilliant leaves tend to eclipse the small red berries that ripen at the same time.

Centrepiece among a spring display of tulips, *Berberis thunbergii atropurpurea* associates well with plants in the warm colour range, from reds through crimson to purple. The shrub retains its browny-purple leaf colour through the summer, but becomes more ruddy in autumn.

ABOVE *Berberis thunbergii* 'Red Chief' flowers in spring

Berberis thunbergii atropurpurea

BARBERRY

Purple foliage, yellow spring flowers,
bright red berries in autumn

There are over a hundred varieties of berberis, many of them outstanding shrubs of all-round interest. Some are deciduous, some evergreen, but all are thorny and all carry flowers within a colour range of cream through yellow to orange.

A single species, *Berberis thunbergii*, has a variety of forms to satisfy the most discerning gardener. The purple-leaved form, *B.t. atropurpurea*, is one of the best purple shrubs. It reaches 1.8m/6ft in height and spread, and looks well at the back of a mixed border, especially one planted with harmonizing hot colours in the range of crimson, red and orange. A dwarf purple variety, *B.t.* 'Atropurpurea Nana', which reaches a height of 60cm/24in, is useful for small gardens. In spring both produce numerous small pendulous yellow flowers which contrast with the developing purple foliage. Small bright red berries ripen in autumn, to coincide with a deepening intensity of colour in the leaves before they fall. The rich purple foliage takes on a reddish tinge, which complements the berries hanging below the leaves.

For the most showy flowers, choose the purple-leaved *B.t.* 'Red Chief'. This has larger flowers than

Berberis thunbergii atropurpurea berries in autumn

B.t. atropurpurea, and the outer bracts are suffused with red. Disappointingly, though, it is not a reliable producer of berries. Another striking purple-leaved berberis is *B.t.* 'Rose Glow'. In this variety the young leaves are mottled with pink and creamy-white patterns, later darkening to purple. Aptly named, the plant appears to glow with a halo of pink from its young shoots. The variegated forms tend to be smaller and less vigorous than the type. 'Rose Glow' grows to 1.5m/5ft.

With their vicious battery of thorns, *B. thunbergii* and its varieties make impenetrable hedging plants. The larger varieties, such as *B.t. atropurpurea*, should be spaced 60cm/24in apart. For a dwarf hedge of *B.t.* 'Atropurpurea Nana', place plants 30cm/12in apart.

• Any soil, provided it is not waterlogged. Sun or part-shade. Propagate by cuttings. Zone 5

ANOTHER BERBERIS TO GROW

Berberis darwinii A good evergreen barberry for a mild climate, *B. darwinii* grows to 2.5m/8ft and is covered in spring with bright orange flowers. The autumn display, of purple berries, is less reliable. Zone 7

Many berberis species are generous producers of berries in autumn. They remain on the shrub well into winter when, as here, they look sensational with a sprinkling of hoar frost. The berries are not always red. There are species with blue berries, others with purple, and some that have a bloom on their surface that makes them quite white.

Buxus sempervirens
COMMON BOX
Aromatic evergreen for hedges and punctuation marks

There is a place for box in every garden. It is the most adaptable of plants and has been used for hedging and topiary for centuries. In some historic gardens the box infrastructure has survived long after the more ephemeral garden plants have vanished.

Left to its own devices and given many years, box makes a small evergreen tree. Its greenish-grey trunk is usually fairly bent and twisted – an indication of its age – and it bears modest but sweet-scented flowers. These are rarely seen on box when it is pruned to shape, which is the way that it is usually grown.

With its small leaves growing densely together to give good coverage all the year round, box is the perfect plant for shaping. It is easily propagated by cuttings, and perhaps its only disadvantage is that it is so slow-growing. If you fancy a box edging to your borders, you will do best to plant rooted cuttings about 15cm/6in high and 15cm/6in apart, but you will have to wait four or five years before they grow together to give any effect, and much longer for any height. Meanwhile you will need to restrain the more vigorous border plants from swamping the baby box.

Box shapes such as cones, cubes, balls and spirals make delightful architectural punctuation marks at strategic points such as the corners of borders, or beside entrances or steps. They can also be grown in pots to be moved around as the mood takes you. Unless you have the patience of Job it would be wise to buy your box shapes ready-made from the nursery. They may be expensive, but the price will be a fair reflection of the years it has taken to create them.

• Any soil. After planting box plants for hedging, trim the top shoots to stimulate further growth

from the base. Prune hard as the hedge develops; it may be discouraging for the gardener to cut back a plant that grows so painfully slowly, but this is vital to encourage compact growth. Do not neglect to feed the plants – preferably with a top-dressing of well-rotted manure – to stimulate growth. Zone 6

OTHER BOXES TO GROW

***Buxus sempervirens* varieties** There are numerous forms of *Buxus sempervirens* with slight distinctions in leaf shape or colour, or in overall habit. *B.s.* 'Suffruticosa' is a dwarf form of the common box, with brighter green leaves, and is ideal as an edging plant or for small topiary shapes; *B.s.* 'Aureovariegata' has leaves mottled with yellow; *B.s.* 'Bullata' (syn. 'Latifolia') is a more loosely spreading shrub with larger leaves; and *B.s.* 'Angustifolia' (syn. 'Longifolia') has larger, oblong leaves. Zone 6

Buxus microphylla This box is good in colder climates, and has the additional advantage that it grows naturally into a compact dome shape. So, provided this is the shape you want, there is no need to prune it. The variety *B.m.* 'Compacta' is a dwarf version, ideal for the rock garden. *B.m.* 'Green Pillow' is another good compact form, with brighter green leaves. Zone 5

Simple but effective. Box topiary shapes grown in containers provide punctuation marks in a tiny urban garden. Untrimmed ivy makes a clever contrast around two of the box structures. Both box and ivy will look much the same in winter, but both need regular trimming – the box to keep its shape and the ivy to ensure that it remains in its juvenile state. Ivies become bulky and the leaves less shapely in their adult phase.

Choisya ternata

MEXICAN ORANGE BLOSSOM

Aromatic evergreen foliage, perfumed white flowers over a long season

Many evergreen shrubs have thick and waxy leaves, to give them some protection from extremes of temperature. Choisya, the Mexican orange blossom, is an exception, with leaves that are thin and sensuously soft. Admittedly, it is not the hardiest of evergreens, but in a temperate area it should come happily through most winters.

In a colder climate choisya can be grown as a wall shrub, and, if you want to take the process a stage further, you can train it flat against the wall. It is quite content to be trained and clipped to shape and it is a pleasure to prune, as the leaves release a strong but pleasant scent, reminiscent of oil of eucalyptus, when bruised or cut.

The flowers of choisya are scented too, but their perfume is quite sweet. They are white and look rather like orange blossom – which is why the plant was given its popular name. The main flush of flowers is in late spring but the shrub sometimes blooms again in autumn.

● Height and spread to 2.5m/8ft. Full sun for maximum flowering, but it will flower in shade. Any well-drained soil. Protect from frosts in cold areas. Propagate by cuttings. Zone 8

Choisya ternata flowers

Choisya ternata in flower in a rather untypical woodland setting. Choisya is not generally regarded as a woodland shrub, but it will thrive in conditions of shade or part-shade. One advantage of this situation is that the surrounding trees will give it protection from frosts.

Clematis species and varieties

An invaluable group of climbers that, between them,
produce flowers all the year round

Clematis are the most versatile of climbers. While no individual clematis has a particularly long flowering season, between them they provide flowers the whole year round. They are invaluable for extending the season of interest of the trees and shrubs through which they are trained. If you select your clematis carefully you can create the illusion that a tree or shrub is coming into flower again long after its own season has ended.

Some of the most useful clematis are those that are relatively late-flowering, coming to a peak towards the end of the summer when many of the star acts in the garden, such as roses, are past their best. The **Viticella group** is especially valuable, offering a range of colours to suit most tastes and garden situations. The Viticellas are characterized by small flowers, many of them bell-shaped. There are also some wonderful eccentrics among them, like 'Purpurea Plena Elegans', with its double flowers like opulently embroidered mauve buttons.

Most subtle among the Viticellas is 'Alba Luxurians', with its wavy white sepals tipped with green. It is too modest in colour to decorate a green-leaved shrub, but it can look magical growing among the purple foliage of the barberry, *Berberis thunbergii atropurpurea*, or a purple form of the smoke bush, *Cotinus coggygria*. Another good white Viticella is the variety 'Huldine'. The flowers are slightly in-turned and have a beautiful silvery-pink sheen.

Try one of the red Viticellas as a contrast to a plain green or white-variegated host plant. 'Abundance' is among the best. It is as free-flowering as its name suggests, with flattish, flowers of a slightly dusty mid-pink. 'Madame Julia Correvon' is another good one, with cupped flowers of a richer pink, and pointed sepals.

Shrubs with yellow or yellow-variegated foliage are well suited as hosts for the darker colours among the Viticellas, particularly those within the purple range, like 'Etoile Violette' or 'Venosa Violacea', which has violet flowers streaked with white. Perhaps the most splendid in colour of all the Viticellas is 'Royal Velours', which has the texture and hue of deep burgundy velvet. It makes a regal complement to any tree or shrub.

The hybrid ***Clematis* × *durandii*** is another useful plant that flowers in late summer. This clematis has flowers of deep blue, many of them with only four sepals, each slightly twisted and with surface corrugations along its length. One of its parents is a herbaceous clematis and so, although it makes sturdy and vigorous growth, it is a weak climber, only reaching a height of about 1.5m/5ft. Its blue flowers make an effective decoration for a yellow-leaved shrub such as *Lonicera nitida* 'Baggesen's Gold'.

The delightful ***Clematis rehderiana*** also comes into flower towards the end of summer, producing masses of diminutive nodding flowers, coloured pale primrose-yellow. This climber will reach 6m/20ft, and if you can get your nose to the flowers you will enjoy their subtle but deliciously sweet scent.

***Clematis* 'Bill Mackenzie'**, a vigorous clematis reaching 7.5m/25ft, has an impressive double act – a spectacular late summer display of medium-small flowers, followed by a mass of fluffy seedheads or 'old man's beard' carried well into winter. The flowers are bright yellow bells with brownish stamens, and

A white clematis weaves together the separate elements in a white and silver planting. The clematis is a Viticella, 'Alba Luxurians', which looks good in the silver-leaved sea buckthorn (*Hippophaë rhamnoides*), planted beside a white-flowered *Buddleja davidii*, with double white leucanthemums and feverfew at their feet.

the sepals are often upturned at the tip. **C. tangutica** is a slightly less vigorous climber with smaller yellow flowers but with seedheads that are just as enduring.

Clematis cirrhosa actually begins to produce its small bell-shaped creamy-yellow flowers (usually mottled with maroon) around midwinter. It then remains in bloom for two or three months. It has attractive feathered foliage, but this is apt to form a dense mat, so *C. cirrhosa* is not suitable for growing through the more delicate shrubs. It is better used to cover the bare trunk of a tree, or the side of an unsightly building.

With any luck, *C. cirrhosa* will still be flowering when **Clematis armandii** comes into bloom, in very early spring. If you judge by its foliage *C. armandii* looks quite unlike any other clematis, with evergreen leaves like dark green leather straps. But when the flowers open they are unmistakably typical of clematis, with four to six petal-like sepals surrounding a crown of anthers. The flowers grow in clusters from buds which develop over the winter at points where the leaves meet the main stem. Typically they are creamy white, waxy in texture and scented sweetly of almonds. But my favourite cultivar is the pale pink one called 'Apple Blossom'. The leaves offer a broad surface area to be attacked by frost, so it is advisable to cover the plant during hard winter weather.

Coinciding with the spring bulbs, **Clematis alpina** has small, nodding flowers, normally blue, but with a pink form called 'Ruby' and a double white called 'White Moth'. One of the best forms is *C.a.* 'Frances Rivis', which has long blue sepals and a prominent white centre. *C. alpina* is another clematis that produces fluffy seedheads. They last throughout the summer and make an attractive association with later climbers such as roses, sweet peas, or later-flowering clematis.

Clematis montana, which blossoms in late spring, has lovely small flowers, from white to dark pink according to the variety. Among the most perfect are *C.m.* 'Tetrarose', which has deep pink flowers with creamy-yellow stamens, and *C.m.* var. *rubens*, which has pink flowers and bronzy-red foliage. If you need a climber to clothe an eyesore in the garden, this is the one for you, because it is extremely vigorous and free-flowering. I offer a note of caution, however, having made a bad mistake in siting a *C. montana* in my own garden. I decided to grow one into the old apple tree which is the centrepiece of the garden. Within five years there were bare stems as thick as my wrist, reaching up into the

A well-matched partnership between *Clematis* 'Prince Charles' and the dwarf *Berberis thunbergii* 'Atropurpurea Nana'. This clematis is similar to 'Perle d'Azur', but it is less vigorous and has smaller flowers.

canopy of the tree, and the apple had stopped bearing flowers and fruit. Bruised by this experience, I would only recommend *C. montana* to clothe a building or a really sturdy tree. It would look effective, for instance, draped through the dense foliage of a conifer such as Leyland cypress.

The clematis with the most spectacular blooms are the **large-flowered hybrids**, most of which flower in mid to late summer. Among them there is a wide diversity of forms and colours ranging from white through pink and mauve to blue and deepest purple. Apart from a few less vigorous varieties, they all climb to about 4.5m/15ft. Collectively they give great opportunities for clever associations with other plants of harmonious or contrasting foliage and flower colour.

The best of the large single white hybrids is *C.* 'Marie Boisselot' (syn. 'Madame le Coultre'). A double variety with flowers like big white pom-poms is *C.* 'Duchess of Edinburgh'. If it blooms a second time in autumn the flowers are single, which is also

Clematis cirrhosa in winter

Clematis 'Bill Mackenzie' in early autumn

the case with other double clematis. C. 'Miss Bateman' is another good white clematis, with contrasting brown stamens.

Among the best of the pinks, C. 'Comtesse de Bouchaud' has abundant medium-sized flowers. I have seen it growing into an apple tree to great effect. For a cooler pink and more star-shaped flowers, C. 'Hagley Hybrid' is a good choice: it associates well with *Rosa glauca*. C. 'Bees' Jubilee' is an improvement on the familiar 'Nelly Moser', offering a generally more richly coloured version of Nelly's rather insipid combination of pale pink with darker pink bars.

Clematis 'Lady Northcliffe' is a good lavender-blue clematis, and ideal for the smaller garden, as it reaches only 2.5m/8ft. C. 'Prince Charles' is another good smaller variety, with exquisite pale blue flowers. It is rather like a miniature version of the magnificent 'Perle d'Azur', everybody's favourite for a vigorous pale blue climber. C. 'H.F. Young' and C. 'Lasurstern' are among the best of the darker blues. I have seen 'Lasurstern' planted in daring combination with the orange-flowered honeysuckle *Lonicera × tellmanniana*. The two climbers flower simultaneously in a startling dazzle of orange and blue.

For a clematis of deep velvety purple, a colour that has overtones of royal occasions and solemn state funerals, choose C. 'Jackmanii Superba'. It is a glorious tone of purple, subtly marked with bars of purple-magenta. There is also a variety called C. 'Jackmanii Rubra', in tones of magenta and pink.

● All clematis do best in alkaline conditions, where there is lime in the soil. There are several points to bear in mind when growing clematis in association with trees and shrubs. Clematis thrive best with their roots shaded from sun, and (in common with most plants), they grow up towards the light. It is best therefore to plant any clematis on the shaded side of the host plant, so that it will grow up and through the host towards the sun. It is also important that the roots of the climber should not have to compete with its host for water and nourishment, so clematis need to be planted outside the sphere of influence of tree roots. As a rough guide, you might estimate the edge of the host's canopy in five years' time and plant the climber there. A cane support, angled into the host plant, will direct its early growth, and you will need to tie the shoots to this cane as they progress upwards. Regular watering, and feeding at weekly intervals in the summer, will give a strong plant that ought to flower in its first year.

There is something of a mystique about the pruning of clematis, but in fact the principles are fairly simple. The main reason for pruning is to encourage growth from the base and to keep the plant within bounds. If left to its own devices it will start growing from the point at which it left off the previous season, and so the most vigorous species can quickly get out of hand. As a rule all clematis will flower on the growth they have made the preceding summer. In the case of late-flowering types the preceding summer is usually the current one. So these are species that may be cut back boldly in late winter; they will flower on the growth they make in the subsequent months. The spring-flowering species also flower on the growth of the preceding summer, but in their case, of course, this is the summer of the previous year. So these species need to be pruned after their spring flowering, to give them the summer to make new growth for next year's flowering. Propagate clematis by cuttings or layering.

The clematis of the Viticella group, C. × *durandii*, C. *rehderiana*, C. 'Bill Mackenzie', C. *tangutica* and all the large-flowered hybrids mentioned are hardy to zone 6; C. *cirrhosa* is hardy to zone 8, C. *armandii* only to zone 9; the species C. *alpina*, 'Ruby' and 'Frances Rivis' are hardy to zone 5, 'White Moth' to zone 3; C. *montana* and its varieties are hardy to zone 5.

A medley of clematis. This is only a small selection from the over 300 varieties available, but they have been chosen to illustrate the range of colours and flower forms that clematis has to offer. The blue-flowered *Clematis × durandii* looks good growing in a yellow-leaved shrub such as *Lonicera nitida* 'Baggesen's Gold', but it is not a vigorous climber and will not reach the upper branches of a tall shrub. *Clematis* 'Huldine', on the other hand, is extremely vigorous and is effective planted with old-fashioned roses. When the rose flowers are finished, the clematis replaces them for several weeks with its own silvery flowers.

C. × *durandii* in *Lonicera nitida* 'Baggesen's Gold'

C. 'Jackmanii Superba'

C. 'Huldine'

C. 'Comtesse de Bouchaud'

C. 'Lady Northcliffe'

C. 'Perle d'Azur'

C. *alpina* 'Frances Rivis'

C. 'Bees' Jubilee'

C. 'Hagley Hybrid'

C. *montana* 'Tetrarose'

C. *armandii* 'Apple Blossom'

Cornus alba 'Elegantissima'

VARIEGATED DOGWOOD

Patterned foliage, creamy-white summer flowers and
wine-red young stems for winter colour

The genus *Cornus* comes in a wide range of shapes
and sizes, from medium-sized trees (pages 28-9) to
lowly ground-cover plants (page 110). The shrubby
species probably have the greatest general appeal and
among them there is a wide diversity of forms. Even
within the species *Cornus alba* there are at least three
varieties very different from each other but of equal
value. I would place *C.a.* 'Elegantissima' very high on
my list of top plants, with *C.a.* 'Sibirica' and *C.a.*
'Spaethii' jostling for space on the pedestal.

'Elegantissima' is an appropriate name-tag for a
plant with such exquisitely decorated leaves. Oval,
with sharply pointed tips, they are mid-green and
patterned with margins of pure white. There is considerable variety among the leaves in width and outline of variegation. As with a fine painting you can
enjoy this foliage at any distance. In close-up it is the
intricate patterns of variegation that appeal. From
further away the patterns merge and the overall
effect is of a bright and slightly shimmering silvery
shrub. As such it is invaluable in the mixed border
and will bring a touch of light to a planting scheme,
especially in contrast with darker shrubs and hedges.

In early summer the shrub bears heads of small
creamy-white flowers. These are attractive enough
in themselves but they tend to merge visually with
the white edging of the leaves and so they are not a
conspicuous feature. Likewise the fruits – this
variety is very shy to produce fruits but when it does
they are white and almost invisible against the
foliage. The white berries are a more prominent
feature on the unvariegated forms of *C. alba*. Not
only do they appear more consistently but they also
contrast effectively with the coppery red of the
autumn leaves in the plain variety.

Cornus alba 'Elegantissima' makes a good host for the more colourful flowers of climbers such as clematis or nasturtiums. I would propose the Viticella clematis 'Venosa Violacea', with its subtle purple and white flowers, as a perfect foil to the white-variegated leaves of the cornus. The deep purple C. × jackmanii would look good too, twined through the cornus foliage.

A star feature of all varieties of C. alba is the coloured bark of the young stems. These are revealed when the leaves fall in autumn and they make an outstanding contribution to the garden in winter. In C.a. 'Elegantissima' they are a deep wine-red.

● Unrestrained, C. alba and its varieties (see below) will reach a height of 2.5m/8ft and a spread of 3.5m/12ft, but you can keep plants within bounds by boldly cutting back in spring. A severe pruning regime is crucial if you want to get the best effects of winter colour from the bark. Remember that it is only the new shoots that colour up. The plant will survive if you cut all new growth back to base wood in spring, but it is prudent to leave one-third of the shoots each year so that it can make a good start when the sap rises. An advantage of severe pruning is that the foliage grows more vigorously on young shoots and you will get larger and more brightly decorated leaves. This shrub is impartial between sun and part-shade, and thrives in any soil. You will often see it planted near water, not only because it enjoys plenty of moisture, but also because its winter colour gives double effect when reflected in water. Propagate by cuttings. Zone 2

OPPOSITE Cornus alba 'Elegantissima' makes a fine backdrop to a handsome terracotta urn. The shrub is amenable to pruning and it can be trained flat against a wall.

RIGHT Cornus alba 'Sibirica', the Westonbirt dogwood, is the variety with the brightest red stems.

OTHER DOGWOODS TO GROW

***Cornus alba* 'Kesselringii'** A dogwood with stems that are such a dark purple-brown that they appear almost black in the thin winter sun. It looks good as part of a mixed planting of cornus and willows with their different stem colours for winter effect. Prune annually in spring, as with other dogwoods grown for stem colour. Zone 2

***Cornus alba* 'Sibirica'** The Westonbirt dogwood is the best of the group for winter colour. The young stems are brilliant scarlet and the leaves colour up well before they fall in autumn. For outstanding winter effect prune severely in spring. Zone 2

***Cornus alba* 'Spaethii'** A form with glorious yellow and green variegated foliage. It looks fine in the mixed border, particularly in association with hot-coloured flowers in the red to yellow range. Pruned down to the ground in spring it will put up young growth with much larger leaves than normal. Zone 2

***Cornus alternifolia* 'Argentea'** A beautiful shrub with silvery variegation, its branches distinctively arranged in tiers. In this respect it resembles the tree *C. controversa* 'Variegata', but the shrub is more compact and the foliage more dense. Height and spread to 6m/20ft. Its slowly developing shape is its virtue, so do not prune, unless to remove dead wood. Zone 3

***Cornus stolonifera* 'Flaviramea'** (syn. *C. sericea* 'Flaviramea') Grown for its young stems of golden yellow which give superb winter colour, especially when grown beside varieties of *C. alba* with red stems to give contrast. If left to its own devices it will grow to the same dimensions as *C. alba*, but like its cousin it will perform best if severely cut back in spring. Zone 2

Corylus avellana 'Contorta'

CORKSCREW HAZEL
Twisted corkscrew branches, catkins in early spring

This is an eccentric shrub, but there is room for one or two eccentrics in most gardens. Its twigs and branches twist into shapes that imply great age. In fact the corkscrew hazel is not necessarily old at all; it is merely a freak variety of the common hazel. It was first spotted growing wild in an English hedge-row in the 1860s, which only goes to show that observation is sometimes all that is needed to discover a new plant. Its twisted stems are seen to best effect in winter when they are bare of leaves. They look especially striking with a stubble of hoar frost, which increases the illusion of wizened old age.

In early spring the branches are hung with tassels of pale khaki-coloured catkins that contrast with the stems. Later the leaves appear, obscuring the twisted branches. They are attractive leaves, rounded and typical of the hazels, and colouring up yellow in autumn. Since the shrub is relatively dull in summer it is a good candidate to decorate with a clematis.

● Height and spread to 4.5m/15ft, which is a little shorter than the common cobnut, *C. avellana*, of which it is a variety. Any soil, sun or part-shade. It may only be conserved by vegetative reproduction, so propagate by cuttings. Zone 5

OTHER HAZELS TO GROW

***Corylus maxima* 'Purpurea'** The purple-leaved filbert is one of the best shrubs for purple foliage, with generously broad leaves of deep purple-brown. The leaves grow larger if you keep the shrub low by coppicing, but then you will miss the purple-tinted catkins, which appear in spring on bare branches, and also the autumn bounty of cobnuts. Height to 6m/20ft, spread 4.5m/15ft. Zone 5

A heavy hoar frost inscribes a white outline to the crazy twisted stems of *Corylus avellana* 'Contorta'. Although it is midwinter the catkins are beginning to form, and within a few weeks the shrub will be decked out in its spring display.

Cotinus coggygria 'Royal Purple'

PURPLE SMOKE BUSH

Purple summer foliage with red autumn tints, fluffy
flower heads in summer, lasting into autumn

The summer foliage of this shrub is a deep velvety
purple, which makes it an excellent choice for the
back of a mixed border. Against this dark backdrop
the inevitably brighter flowers of the border will
shine out. In autumn the leaves turn to fiery red.

The flowers from which this cotinus earns its
name of 'smoke bush' are produced by mature
plants. Individually tiny, the flowers grow together
in a diaphanous plume. In the case of 'Royal Purple'
they are reddish brown. The candyfloss-like structure of the inflorescences lasts into autumn, while
the flowers turn into tiny fruits. Unfortunately, if
you are to get full value from the foliage, you have to
dispense with the flowers. The leaves are fresher and
larger on young wood, and for the best foliage you
should prune the shrub back to base each spring.
But in doing so you sacrifice its ability to flower.

• Height and spread to 3m/10ft. Sun or part-shade.
Any soil; for best autumn colour, should not be
richly manured. Propagate by cuttings. Zone 5

OTHER COTINUS TO GROW

***Cotinus* 'Flame'** and **C. 'Grace'** are both larger
than *C. coggygria*, with bigger, bolder leaves. *C.*
'Flame' has green foliage that colours in autumn to a
bright orange-red. 'Grace' has purplish-red leaves
that turn orange-red. Zone 5

So dark that it appears
black in contrast with the
yellow golden rod
(*Solidago*) planted beside
it, this *Cotinus coggygria*
'Royal Purple' has been
cut back to ground level
each spring. Pruning
ensures that the plant
does not grow too big. It
also stimulates it to
produce larger leaves.

Cotoneaster horizontalis

Scarlet autumn foliage and red berries that
last into winter

The branches of this shrub radiate from the main
stems like the bones of a fish. Collectively the stems
spread out flat from the centre like a fan – a very
colourful fan in autumn when the leaves colour up
to a bright scarlet to match the red berries that hug
the outline of the 'fishbone'. In a warm climate this
cotoneaster is evergreen. Where it is colder the
leaves fall in winter, but the berries remain on the
leafless skeleton.

Its growth pattern makes this cotoneaster an
excellent plant for growing against a wall. It will
form naturally a fan of up to 1.8m/6ft in height and
spread. Its radiating habit makes it useful for ground
cover too and it is ideal for masking an eyesore like a
drain cover. Again, very little maintenance is needed,
short of the occasional tidying up with secateurs to
remove any branches that refuse to lie flat.

In the floral department this cotoneaster is a bit
of a disappointment. You would be forgiven for not
noticing the tiny pink cups produced in midsummer; they are, however, irresistible to bees.

• A very forgiving plant, that will survive in any soil,
however poor. Sun or part-shade. Fallen berries will
produce seedlings which may be transplanted.
Otherwise propagate by cuttings. Zone 6

OTHER COTONEASTERS TO GROW

Cotoneaster is a large genus, having over fifty species
and many more varieties with widely different uses
in the garden. The main feature that they have in
common is a fecund production of berries – usually
red, but there are some yellow-berried varieties
available. They range in habit from further prostrate
species to small trees.

Cotoneaster horizontalis in autumn

Cotoneaster 'Cornubia' A small tree, up to 6m/20ft
in height, with arching branches which are loaded in
early summer with clusters of white flowers. In
autumn the branches sag under their harvest of red
berries. The leaves, larger than many others of the
genus, are semi-evergreen. Zone 6

Cotoneaster dammeri A prostrate species that
spreads out to 1.8m/6ft at a height of only
45cm/18in. Its deciduous leaves colour scarlet in
autumn. Inconspicuous white flowers are followed
by waxy red berries. Zone 5

Repeat performances by *Fothergilla major*. In spring the modest-looking flowers are powerhouses of scent. In this shaded situation the leaves turn yellow in autumn, not red as they might have done in full sun.

Fothergilla major
Cream-coloured scented flowers in spring, colourful foliage in autumn

Fothergillas produce small flowers, rather like powder puffs, in spring. Cream-coloured, they consist of a mass of stamens without petals and produce a strong scent. They appear on bare stems before the leaves open. Fothergillas make good companions for other acid-loving and spring-flowering shrubs, such as the smaller rhododendron species and camellias. After the flowers have passed, *Fothergilla major* (syn. *F. monticola*) makes an inconspicuous, spreading shrub with rounded leaves not unlike those of the related witch hazel *(Hamamelis)*. In autumn the foliage comes into its own, colouring brightly before it drops. The autumn tints appear to be influenced by the amount of sun that reaches the leaves. Parts of

the fothergilla that are in full shade tend to colour to pure yellow. In sun the leaves may assume patches of scarlet, so the overall effect of the plant in autumn is of a burning bush, glowing with red and gold.

• Height to 2.5m/8ft, spread 1.8m/6ft. Requires lime-free, acid soil with plenty of humus. Suited to open woodland conditions of part-shade. Propagate by cuttings. Zone 5

ANOTHER FOTHERGILLA TO GROW

Fothergilla gardenii The witch alder is the fothergilla to buy if you have a small garden, as it will not exceed 90cm/36in in height or spread. Like its larger relation it requires acid soil and part-shade. Despite its small size, the plant has flowers and leaves that are almost identical to those of *F. major*. Zone 5

An informal area of woodland. The trunk of an oak would normally be quite dark in summer, shaded by its dense canopy of leaves. But this one has been lightened by the bright-leaved ivy *Hedera helix* 'Goldheart' planted at its base. Given free rein, this ivy will shin up into the lower branches of the tree and the heart-shaped immature leaves, seen here, will give way to the mature phase. At this stage the climber becomes more bushy in its upper reaches and gives rise to flowers and fruit. Ivy does not normally damage a healthy tree, unless its foliage cuts out light from the leaves of the host, in which case it should be cut back.

Hedera helix 'Goldheart'

GOLDHEART IVY

Evergreen foliage with a bright yellow
and green pattern

The whole point of gardening, it seems to me, is to tame nature. However much we wish to cultivate the 'wild' look in our gardens, this involves a degree of selection of desirable plants and the suppression of the less desirable ones. Here, in the ivies, is a genus of plants that is the epitome of wildness. Think of ivy and you think of neglect: overgrown gardens choked by rampant ivy, ivy-clad ruins, trees strangled by a straitjacket of dense ivy. And yet if you take care with the selection of plants and with pruning and training, ivy can be tamed to work for you. With imaginative treatment, it becomes a most sophisticated and adaptable plant, while still retaining something of an air of wildness.

For a start, ivy is almost infinitely variable. Countless strains have been selected and named, according to their distinctive leaf colour or shape, or to their pattern of variegation. *Hedera helix* 'Goldheart' (more properly called 'Oro di Bogliasco') is an attractive variety, with its central pattern of bright yellow, framed with green, but I might equally well recommend others, such as 'Buttercup' (overall yellow), or 'Glacier' (grey-green, with frosted white margins). One curious feature of the ivies is that they remain variable, even when a desirable strain has been selected. The chances are that your *H.h.* 'Goldheart' will have slightly different patterns of variegation from your neighbour's. Even as it grows it may change so that you have different leaf patterns on the same plant. Also, the plant changes character when it enters its adult phase. The adult ivy is more bushy and less clinging, and its leaves become less 'ivy-shaped' and more rounded. Only the adult ivy carries flowers and fruit. Growing ivies is an adventure, like a lucky dip.

The simplest way to use ivy is to grow it up a wall or fence. It will grow tightly against the surface, with no loose growth to sway around in wind, and make a valuable contribution to the vertical garden. You can regard it as a background against which to grow an outer layer of climbers such as clematis or even roses. *H.h.* 'Goldheart' makes a wonderful background for blue or purple clematis such as *Clematis alpina* (spring-flowering), *C.* 'Lasurstern' (summer-flowering), and Viticella clematis such as 'Etoile Violette' or 'Royal Velours' (flowering in late summer). It is perfectly easy to grow such climbers together, provided that their roots are well separated so that they do not compete for nourishment. Simply plant the ivy to fan out radially from the base and place the clematis at least 90cm/36in to the side away from

Some ivies, while remaining 'evergreen', give autumn colour. *Hedera helix* 'Gracilis', shown here, is one of them.

Hedera helix 'Marginata Major'

the sun. This way the clematis will grow across the ivy towards the light; unlike the ivy, it needs wires to support it and the occasional tying in to ensure that it grows in the desired direction.

Ivy is equally happy grown as ground cover, but as such it may be so successful that nothing much can be grown with it. Bulbs are an exception, and snowdrops and daffodils may survive happily under a carpet of ivy, with their flowers and foliage reaching up in the appropriate season. Ivy's tolerance of dry shade makes it a very useful ground cover under trees, even conifers. Here, however, it has one limitation: the variegated forms, of which *H.h.* 'Goldheart' is one, need sunlight to make them colour up well. In deep shade it would be better to select pure green forms with interesting leaf shapes: a good example is *H.h.* 'Merion Beauty', which has leaves shaped like those of an acer.

Hedera helix 'Conglomerata'

For lovers of the eccentric, there is a form of the common ivy that is neither climbing nor ground-covering, but which stands independently as a small shrub. This is *H.h.* 'Conglomerata'. It is an admirable curiosity, will puzzle your visitors, and makes an appealing evergreen mound. If you like the idea of ivy in three dimensions, you can make a solid shape by growing a climbing ivy on a wire frame.

You might also consider tinkering with ivy in two dimensions. I was so taken with the idea in a magazine photograph that I took my secateurs and went straight into the garden and cut out the shape of a hand in a fan of ivy growing against the wall. This light-hearted joke took no more than half an hour. Within a few weeks the ivy had regenerated and filled the gaps. So you can use a wall of ivy as a drawing slate, the beauty of it being that nature eventually wipes the slate clean – as it always does.

Hedera helix 'Glacier'

The crude shape of a hand has been cut into a broad-leaved ivy, *Hedera algeriensis* 'Gloire de Marengo', growing on a stone wall. Finer effects can be achieved with small-leaved ivies.

- *Hedera helix* varieties will reach a height and spread of 9m/30ft on suitable supports. Any soil, sun or shade. Zone 5

OTHER IVIES TO GROW

Hedera algeriensis 'Gloire de Marengo' (sometimes called *H. canariensis* 'Gloire de Marengo') An outstanding large-leaved variegated ivy, which is not reliably hardy and so is often grown as a house plant. It has red stems and the leaves are dark green, broken with patterns of grey-green and with margins of white. Makes good ground cover in a mild climate. Grows to 3.5m/12ft. Zone 7

Hedera colchica The Persian ivy has much larger leaves than *H. helix*, with several variegated forms. *Hedera colchica* 'Sulphur Heart' has patterning similar to that of *H. helix* 'Goldheart' on leaves up to 25cm/10in long. This ivy grows rapidly, to a maximum height of around 9m/30ft. Zone 6

Hedera colchica 'Sulphur Heart'

Hydrangea quercifolia in summer

Hydrangea quercifolia

OAK-LEAVED HYDRANGEA

Late summer flowers, interesting foliage that colours
to deep red and purple in autumn

All the hydrangeas give great value with their generous heads of flowers, usually carried in late summer, a season when relatively few flowering shrubs are in action. This one has the additional merit of outstanding foliage. The lobed leaves are, as the name suggests, reminiscent of oak leaves. In autumn they colour to deep shades of red and purple. Some of them remain on the shrub through the winter, bringing a little much-wanted colour to the garden. These old leaves are pushed off by the fresh bright green growth in spring.

The flowers of *Hydrangea quercifolia* are more oblong than the globular heads of the familiar mopheaded hydrangeas. The individual florets are pure white, but the unopened buds give the flower heads a hint of green. The flower heads tend to flop under their own weight, more so when they are weighed down by rain. In fact the habit of the whole plant is a little droopy, and it may need support. I have seen *H. quercifolia* trained against a wall, to great effect. One of the best varieties is the double-flowered *H.q.* 'Snowflake'.

Hydrangea macrophylla in autumn

● Height and spread to 2m/7ft. Like other hydrangeas *H. quercifolia* thrives in part-shade and hates its roots to become dry. Any soil. Zone 5

OTHER HYDRANGEAS TO GROW

***Hydrangea arborescens* 'Grandiflora'** A lovely mopheaded shrub with huge greeny-white flowers. Zone 3

Hydrangea macrophylla The colours of the popular Hortensia mopheads vary according to the acidity of the soil. Good blues only occur naturally on acid soils. On alkaline soils, if you are desperate for blue flowers, you can treat the plants regularly with a proprietary solution. Good varieties include sky-blue 'Gentian Dome' ('Enziandom'), 'Générale Vicomtesse de Vibraye', which ranges from rose-red to bright blue, and 'Maréchal Foch', which can vary from deep pink to dark blue. One of the best features of these hydrangeas is that the flowers die gracefully. They fade on the plant, without withering, and in the process assume a progression of rich tints. If you cut the flower heads during this fading process and dry them off, these colours are often preserved. Zone 6

Hydrangea sargentiana The special merit of this species lies in the foliage, which is like dark green velvet. The flower heads are pale blue. Zone 8

Complementary colours. The sky-blue flowers of *Hydrangea macrophylla* 'Gentian Dome' make a strong contrast against the orange autumn foliage of *Acer japonicum* 'Vitifolium'. The acer will soon shed its leaves, but the hydrangea flowers will die slowly and gracefully. First the blue tint will discolour slightly and fade to purple. Gradually the flowers will brown off and become brittle, but they will never look unsightly, and it is not necessary to remove them until new growth begins in spring.

Mahonia × *media* 'Lionel Fortescue' flowers in winter

Mahonia × *media*

Evergreen foliage, scented yellow winter flowers,
purple fruit bunches in summer

The multiple flower spikes of *Mahonia* × *media* light
up the garden in midwinter like bright yellow can-
delabra. They cast a delicate scent on the air, giving a
happy illusion that spring is not far behind.

Even without its lovely winter flowers, *Mahonia* ×
media would be well worth growing as an architectural shrub, and for its handsome evergreen foliage.
The leaves are arranged in rosettes, each leaf divided
into numerous leaflets which are brittle and prickly
and reminiscent of holly leaves. The plant has a

Mahonia aquifolium flowers in spring

Mahonia aquifolium berries in summer

somewhat stiff, erect habit and the flowers grow from the centre of the leaf rosettes. In addition to the flowers and foliage, the mahonias have a third string to their bow, the purple-blue bunches of fruit that follow the flowers and decorate the shrub throughout the summer.

There are several excellent named forms of *Mahonia × media*, including 'Charity', which grows to a height of 3m/10ft and spread of 2.5m/8ft; its leaves are up to 45cm/18in long, with long prickly leaflets. *M. × m.* 'Lionel Fortescue' has broader leaflets with upright flowers. These and other mahonias may be pruned after flowering to contain their size for the smaller garden.

• Any well-drained soil, sun or shade. Zone 8/9

OTHER MAHONIAS TO GROW

Mahonia aquifolium The Oregon grape is a less striking shrub than *M. × media*, growing only to a height of 1.5m/5ft. Its yellow flowers appear in dense clusters in spring – later than the other mahonias – and they are followed by generous bunches of the purple fruits that earn the plant its popular name. Most seed-raised plants sold as *M. aquifolium* are hybrids, which tend to send up numerous suckers from their roots, and may colonize a shady corner of the garden within a few years. Zone 5

Mahonia japonica One of the parents of the hybrid *M. × media*, with many of its attractive features. However, it is more bushy in habit and less upright, with drooping flower spikes and more spindly leaves. It comes into flower a few weeks later than *M. × media* and so you can extend the flowering season by planting the two together. The hybrid inherits its more rigid characteristics from its other parent, *M. lomariifolia*, which is a magnificent tall and erect shrub, but not reliably hardy. Zone 7

The passion flower produces flowers over such a long period that by the end of the season the fruits derived from earlier flowers coincide with the latest blooms. Winter frosts put an end to this production line. This climber will benefit from the protection offered by a house wall.

Passiflora caerulea

PASSION FLOWER

Decorative foliage, exotic summer flowers, colourful autumn fruits

The passion flower is so called because the parts of its wide-open flowers can be taken to represent the Passion of Christ. The frill of striped filaments around the centre, for instance, can be read as a symbol for the crown of thorns. Whatever the interpretation, *Passiflora caerulea* is a most dramatic flower, exotic in all parts, with leaves divided into five finger-like leaflets, and bright orange fruits ripening in autumn and hanging heavy on the climber as it begins to die back in winter. Flowers are produced over a long season, and continue to appear while the fruits are ripening.

• Height and spread up to 6m/20ft on a sunny wall or trellis. Originating in South America, *P. caerulea* is not hardy in an area that has cold winters. To be on the safe side you may elect to grow it in a conservatory, but it is so vigorous that it may become matted unless you cut it back hard every winter. Any soil. Propagate by seed or cuttings. Zone 8/9

Phlomis fruticosa

JERUSALEM SAGE

Evergreen foliage, yellow flowers over a long period in summer, winter seedheads

Jerusalem sage grows wild in the rocky limestone scrub of the Mediterranean, where it is hot and dry in summer. The more closely you can match these conditions in the garden, the better it will perform for you. In a sunny spot it will put out heads of yellow flowers throughout the early summer. Hooded, like those of the true sages, the flowers are arranged in loosely circular flower heads and their yellow hue picks up a hint of the same colour as the

Phlomis fruticosa in early summer

Phlomis fruticosa in winter

pale grey-green tint of the foliage. The leaves are narrow, soft and slightly hairy and remain on the plant throughout the winter.

The individual flower heads drop off in time, but the rounded seedheads remain. Leave these on the plant and they will be rewarding in the winter. By then they will have dried into brittle, brownish pepperpots which look attractive with a seasoning of hoar frost. You might pick a few for the everlasting flower display.

Like other yellow-flowered shrubs, this phlomis looks good associated with flowers in the blue to lilac range. It is wonderful underplanted with the clear blue *Geranium* 'Johnson's Blue'.

• Height up to 1.5m/5ft, spread to 1.8m/6ft, but it can be pruned in spring to make a smaller shrub. Requires full sun. Any soil, including poorly nourished, stony ground. Propagate by cuttings. Zone 8

ANOTHER PHLOMIS TO GROW

Phlomis russeliana A herbaceous perennial, reaching a height and spread of 90cm/36in before dying back in winter. The individual flowers are similar in form and colour to those of *P. fruticosa,* but the rounded flower heads are spaced along the stem in tiers, with gaps of about 8cm/3in between them. These make dramatic seedheads in winter. Propagate by division in spring or autumn. Zone 5

Pieris 'Forest Flame'

Evergreen with scented flowers in spring and colourful young foliage through the summer

There is a time in late spring when the two star features of pieris coincide. Before the hanging bunches of creamy pearl-like flowers have passed over, the stems are beginning to glow red with new leafy growth. The bright young scarlet leaves sprout from the tips of the shoots and the shrub remains ablaze with colour for much of the summer.

Pieris 'Forest Flame' is one of several hybrids related to *P. japonica,* all of which perform this double act with flowers and foliage. *P.* 'Firecrest' is a hybrid with similar flame-red young shoots. In *P.* 'Bert Chandler' the young foliage is salmon-pink, fading to cream before assuming its mature green coloration. There is also an attractive variegated form of *P. japonica* which has leaves edged with white. It is very slow-growing.

• Height to 3.5m/12ft, spread 2.5m/8ft. A shrub for the open woodland, requiring acid soil and rich humus. Propagate by cuttings. Zone 8

Pieris 'Forest Flame' in late spring

A double act by *Pyracantha coccinea*. In summer (ABOVE LEFT) the cream flowers harmonize with the amber rose 'Climbing Lady Hillingdon'. By autumn (ABOVE RIGHT) the rose is bare but the pyracantha is still ablaze with berries.

Pyracantha coccinea

FIRETHORN

Evergreen with red autumn berries following creamy-white summer flowers

As a shrub that has something to show for itself in every month of the year, *Pyracantha coccinea* takes a lot of beating. Its greatest glory is the blaze of bright red berries that sets the garden alight in autumn. The berries last well into winter, a tempting larder for the birds you would have thought, but fortunately they tend to leave them alone until their more regular sources of food have been used up.

The prolific flowers appear in midsummer and we would pay more attention to them if they did not coincide with the more conspicuous stars of the border such as roses, delphiniums, clematis and poppies. The flowers are cream-coloured and tiny

but they grow in dense swathes that cover the plant. A clever association that I have seen is the rambler rose 'Wedding Day' climbing through a mature wall-trained pyracantha. The creamy-white flowers of the rose open at the same time as those of the shrub and again in the autumn the rose hips coincide with the pyracantha's berries. In both seasons, the two plants display similar features that are just different enough to create interest.

Although perfectly satisfactory as free-standing shrubs, pyracanthas are often trained flat to cover a wall. The evergreen foliage of small, finely toothed leaves makes an attractive background all the year round and it provides a good contrast when the flowers and berries hold sway.

To train a pyracantha as an espalier, you will need to fix horizontal wires against the wall or fence, some 30cm/12in apart. Start with a young pot-grown plant with a straight stem, and plant it at least 30cm/12in away from the wall to give the roots a chance to find moisture. Wear gloves and handle the plant with respect, as it has long, sharp thorns along the stems. Keep the leader vertical and tie in the laterals horizontally, cutting out any that cannot be made to lie flat. As it grows, tie in new laterals and maintain the leader until it reaches the required height. At that point, trim the tip to arrest further vertical growth.

Pyracantha can be grown as a hedge too, and here its thorns can be considered an advantage as they help to make it an impenetrable barrier. However, the display of flowers and berries is bound to be reduced in proportion to the amount of trimming that is needed to keep the hedge tidy.

• As a free-standing shrub, height and spread to 6m/20ft. A spread of up to 9m/30ft can be achieved on a wall-trained espalier. Pyracanthas are tolerant of any soil and will flourish in sun or part-shade. Propagate by cuttings of the current year's shoots in late summer. Trim trained plants, including hedges, in summer. Zone 6

OTHER PYRACANTHAS TO GROW

Pyracantha coccinea 'Lalandei' This is the form of *P. coccinea* that is most commonly available. It is more vigorous and larger in leaf and berry than the species. The berries are light red, verging on orange. Zone 6

Pyracantha 'Mohave' A disease-resistant hybrid with red berries. Zone 6

Pyracantha 'Orange Glow' If you aspire to bright orange berries, this is the hybrid for you. The berries are so bright that you could use the plant to bring a little autumn cheer to a part-shaded corner. Zone 6

Rosa glauca
Grey foliage, single pink flowers in summer, red autumn hips

A rose grown for its dark grey foliage suffused with pink, *Rosa glauca* (syn. *R. rubrifolia*) has the added bonus of a magnificent display of deep red hips in autumn. It originated as a wild rose in Central Europe, and like many wild roses it has flowers that are modest but delightful. They are single, of a shade of pink that echoes the traces of pink in the leaves, with yellow stamens. Compared to the concentration of hips in autumn, the flowers are sparsely scattered over the shrub at any one time, but they do appear over a relatively long period in summer.

I have seen this rose grown very effectively in an autumn red border, with great sprays of red hips arching over penstemons and the deep red *Dahlia*

Rosa glauca flower

Rosa glauca hips in autumn

Rosa moyesii flowers in summer

Rosa moyesii hips in winter

'Bishop of Llandaff'. But in this red colour combination, the earlier pink flowers would look unsightly; it is a challenge to a gardener's ingenuity to arrange the planting so that the pink flowers associate well with a pink or blue partner in summer, only to be replaced by a bright red partner to accompany the autumn hips. The leaves alone, however, make an attractive foil for almost any plant.

If it is allowed a free rein, *R. glauca* will grow into a bushy shrub. But it is a forgiving plant and in a small garden it can be pruned right back so that fresh young growth begins again from the base in spring.

• Height and spread 2m/7ft. Leaf colour is better in sun; any soil. Propagate by cuttings. Zone 4

Rosa moyesii

Single scarlet flowers in summer, followed by bright red autumn hips

Grown for its magnificent hips, *Rosa moyesii* is a large shrub with a height and spread of up to 4.5m/15ft. This species rose is clearly unsuitable for the small garden, but its hybrid *R.* 'Geranium' is more containable at about 2.5m/8ft.

The species *R. moyesii* itself is a magnificent sight in autumn, with long branches arching under the weight of its bright red hips, which grow in clusters down each branch. *R. moyesii* has elongated hips, swollen at the base, while those of *R.* 'Geranium' are more rounded. Both are a vivid red, and last well on the shrub provided that the local birds do not develop an appetite for them; this seems to vary with the district.

There can be no fruit, of course, without flowers, but in this rose the flowers are sometimes regarded as a poor relation. This is rather unfair, as the single flowers are handsome, if small in proportion to the plant, and short-lived. In the species and in *R.* 'Geranium' they are a rich blood-red, but in the hybrid *R.* 'Highdownensis' they are pink.

• Will grow on any soil, though shallow chalk needs good preparation, with ample compost dug in to sustain the deep roots. Sun or part-shade. Propagate by cuttings. Zone 6

Rosa rugosa
Crinkled foliage, scented flowers throughout the summer, large red autumn hips

The majority of roses, of course, are grown for their flowers. There are others in which the hips are the strong suit. Others again are chosen for their foliage. In the Rugosa roses all three features, flowers, hips and foliage, are of value in the garden.

The Latin word *rugosa* means wrinkled, and refers to the slightly rough texture of the leaves that characterizes the group. This roughness is due to the slight depression of the veins below the surface. The leaves are resistant to diseases to which many roses are prone, such as black spot and mildew. In my experience they never need spraying, unless against aphids. A further feature of the foliage, unusual in a rose, is the good (albeit short-lived) autumn colour. For a short time the leaves go quite yellow.

It is the colour and form of the flowers that distinguish the different members of the group. The species *Rosa rugosa* itself has flowers of a clear magenta-pink. If you find this hue a little harsh you might prefer to go for the white form, 'Alba'. For a

Rosa rugosa hips in winter

Towards the end of the summer, late flowers on Rugosa roses often coincide with hips derived from earlier flowers. This example is 'Fru Dagmar Hastrup'. The earliest hips endure and the late ones catch up with them so that by late autumn the hip-bearing Rugosas are a mass of colour.

Rosa rugosa 'Alba' in summer

double white, choose the deliciously scented 'Blanc Double de Coubert'. 'Roseraie de l'Haÿ' is a double mauve, the colour of a bishop's cassock and is also beautifully scented. 'Fru Dagmar Hastrup' has exquisite single flowers of a pale shell-pink. All the Rugosas are repeat-flowering.

With some, but by no means all, of the Rugosas, the flowers give rise to fat and succulent red hips. The best plants for hips are *R. rugosa* itself, and *RR. rugosa* 'Alba', 'Scabrosa' and 'Fru Dagmar Hastrup'.

● Height and spread 2m/7ft, though these roses can be kept pruned to a more compact size. Sun or light shade, any soil. Suitable to be grown as a loose hedge. Salt-resistant, so suitable for seaside gardens. Propagate by cuttings. *R. rugosa* is hardy to zone 2; 'Alba', 'Blanc Double de Coubert', 'Roseraie de l'Haÿ and 'Fru Dagmar Hastrup', are all hardy to zone 4.

Rosa Floribunda Group

Multiple blooms over a long period

The Floribundas are some of the most useful roses, not only because they flower so generously, with several blooms on a single stem, but also because they often remain in flower over such a long period.

Rosa 'Iceberg' is one of the most popular of the Floribunda roses, and deservedly so, because of its exceptionally long flowering season. Its first flush of pure white flowers coincides with the peak rose season of midsummer. Provided that you keep it deadheaded, it continues to flower abundantly into autumn and will even produce buds intermittently until midwinter. It will reach a height of 1.5m/5ft and spread of 90cm/36in. There is also a climbing variety, equally reliable in performance, which reaches a height of 3m/10ft.

Rosa 'Iceberg'

If your taste runs to a rose of an outrageously vivid red, then *R.* 'Eye Paint' may be the one for you. The single flowers are scarlet, with a pure white centre that makes the colour all the more intense. Although this rose does not flower over such an extended season, it offers a second performance in autumn when it is covered with a mass of small vermilion hips. It is a vigorous rose, making a dense shrub of 1.5m/5ft in height and spread.

Another outstanding white Floribunda is 'Margaret Merril'. Like 'Iceberg' it produces trusses of well-formed pure white flowers, which can be identified by their pinkish stamens. As an additional attraction it has a lovely scent. On the down side, though, its flowering season is not so long, and it does not stand up very well to wet weather. If you have space, you might consider growing 'Iceberg' and 'Margaret Merril' together, so you can enjoy the longevity of the one and the fragrance of the other.

• Floribundas do best in full sun and rich soil. Zone 6

RIGHT An eyeful of pure colour. *Rosa* 'Eye Paint' is one of the most powerful scarlet roses – not one for the faint-hearted. It has a second innings (ABOVE) with vermilion hips in autumn. It looks especially good when planted in quantity in a larger garden.

Rosmarinus officinalis

ROSEMARY

Aromatic evergreen leaves, blue spring flowers

There is no need to confine rosemary to the herb garden. It will hold its own in the mixed border in association with more obviously glamorous shrubs and perennials. It is best placed beside a path where you will catch the fragrance as you brush past. The small, pointed, aromatic leaves are held all the year round. They are greyish green, paler on the underside, and release their scent when you run them through your hand.

In a mild season the flowers begin to appear in winter and extend well into the spring. They are modest in size but appear in profusion. In the common form of rosemary they are rather insipid in colour, a pale blue that tends to merge into the foliage. It is worth taking the trouble to seek out the form 'Benenden Blue', which is sometimes also listed as 'Collingwood Ingram'. This has flowers of a more full-blooded blue, and darker foliage. It looks well with a spring-flowering variety of ceanothus behind it, and an underplanting of blue spring bulbs such as chionodoxas. There is also a form, *R. officinalis* var. *albiflorus*, with white flowers.

• Height and spread 1.8m/6ft. Being a plant of Mediterranean origin, it demands full sun and a mild climate, though in colder areas it can be grown in a pot and moved into shelter for the winter. It needs well-drained soil. Rosemary has a tendency to become leggy, and it is good practice to prune shoots back to half their length in spring. In mild areas it is possible to grow rosemary as a hedge, but it is hard to keep it tidy. Propagate by cuttings. Zone 8/9

A well-placed pair of *Rosmarinus officinalis*, beside a flight of steps. You can hardly avoid brushing against them, so releasing the scent.

Rubus phoenicolasius

JAPANESE WINEBERRY

Decorative flowers and fruits in early and late summer, arching red stems for winter colour

This rubus arrived in my garden as a chance seedling, hitching a ride with another plant that I had bought at a nursery. Now I would not be without it. It has something interesting to offer all the year round. Its star performance is in winter when it reveals its long, arching stems, bare of leaves but covered along their length by a stubble of fine thorns, rather like a moss rose. These stems are reddish brown in colour, glowing orange when they catch the light of the low winter sun.

In spring and summer the stems are masked with leaves and it is the clusters of developing flower buds that demand our attention. Red and bristly like the stems, the buds are slightly sticky to the touch. They open briefly to reveal the small star-shaped white

LEFT The curious little flower of *Rubus phoenicolasius*. The buds, which have sticky bristles, open for a day or two to allow the flowers to be fertilized. Then they close again to protect the developing fruit (ABOVE).

flowers. Bees go about their work of fertilization and then, curiously, the buds close up again to cover the developing fruits. At this point it is prudent to drape the plant with netting, because when the buds re-open to reveal the fruits they are irresistible to birds. The fruits are shaped like blackberries, their near relations, but they are bright scarlet. They are delicious to eat but if, like the Japanese, you grow them for the table, you need to have a modest appetite. A bush will only feed a family for a single dessert.

• Height to 2.5m/8ft, spread to 3m/10ft. Sun or part-shade, any soil. Left to its own devices the plant will make an untidy bush. It is better to train it flat against a wall, tying the stems against wires to make a loose fan; cut out from the base those stems that grow away from the wall. Each spring cut out about one-third of the stems to encourage new growth. Easily propagated by layering, cuttings or seed. Look out for self-seeded plants, spread by birds. Zone 6

OTHER RUBUS TO GROW

Rubus biflorus Another winter performer, grown for its stems. However, in this rubus the stems are a silvery white, the colour coming from a white bloom overlaying stems of a pale greenish pink. The stems are upright, with branches coming off them at right angles. The general effect is of a tangled white bird-cage. Zone 7

Rubus cockburnianus Similar to *R. biflorus*, with white stems conspicuous in winter, but the stems are arching, like those of *R. phoenicolasius*, and the white bloom overlays a reddish-brown base colour. In summer the plant produces grey-green ferny foliage, but flowers and fruit are insignificant. Height and spread to 4.5m/15ft. Zone 6

Rubus phoenicolasius in winter, with *Mahonia japonica*

Tropaeolum speciosum

FLAME CREEPER

Brilliant red summer flowers followed by
colourful fruits in autumn

There are gardeners who baulk at bright red flowers
but make an exception for this vivid red nasturtium.
Given the delicate scale of the flowers and leaves it is
surprising how far it can shin up a host plant. It
makes drooping curtains of scarlet up to 4.5m/15ft
above the ground. It needs a supporting plant where
the stems or leaves are close together, and nothing is
better for this purpose than topiary yew or box. The
intense red flowers of the tropaeolum look sensational against this dark green background. And the
informality of the creeper makes a pleasing contrast
with the stiff regularity of the topiary.

In autumn the flame creeper produces blue berries, this colour made all the more intense by the
fringe of faded red flower bracts that surround
them. The first frosts wipe out all vestiges of the
plant above the ground, but its underground rhi-
zome survives over winter.

• Any soil, full sun. Propagate by division of roots in
spring. Zone 7

The scarlet flowers of
Tropaeolum speciosum (RIGHT)
give rise to brilliant blue
berries (ABOVE).

Viburnum opulus flowers in late spring

Viburnum opulus

GUELDER ROSE

Attractive foliage, white spring flowers,
bright red autumn berries

A classic dual-purpose shrub, *Viburnum opulus* has large white flower heads, rather like hydrangea flowers, in late spring, followed by brilliant red berries in autumn. In between times the deciduous foliage is a good feature, the leaves being lobed rather like those of the field maple.

The shrub makes a height of 4.5m/15ft, and if space is tight you should consider *V.o.* 'Compactum', which is identical in all other respects but only reaches a height of 1.8m/6ft. For yellow berries, choose *V.o.* 'Xanthocarpum'.

Another very different variety of the same plant is *V.o.* 'Roseum' (syn. 'Sterile'). This has spherical flower heads like creamy-white bobbles. Being sterile, it has the disadvantage of not bearing berries. However, it looks wonderful in late spring growing

next to plants with flowers of contrasting form. The best juxtaposition I have seen is with another good viburnum, *V. plicatum* 'Mariesii'.

• Any soil, sun or part-shade. Propagate by cuttings. Zone 3

OTHER VIBURNUMS TO GROW

The viburnums are a large and invaluable genus of shrubs. Some of the best of them give good value in winter.

Viburnum × bodnantense 'Dawn' This slightly ungainly and lanky deciduous shrub produces its first flowers in late summer, when they are hardly noticeable in comparison with all the summer splendours that are still around. But when it is still

Viburnum opulus berries in autumn

Viburnum plicatum 'Pink Beauty' in summer

Viburnum × *bodnantense* 'Dawn' in winter

flowering in full force in midwinter, after all its leaves have fallen, it is another matter. The flowers are pale pink and gloriously scented. Zone 7

***Viburnum plicatum* 'Mariesii'** An outstanding shrub, with gracefully tiered branches which are dressed in summer with large white flower heads. In autumn the leaves turn a coppery red and there is sometimes a crop of small scarlet berries. In *V.p.* 'Pink Beauty' the flowers are tinged with pink. Height 2.5m/8ft, spread 4.5m/15ft. Zone 5

Viburnum tinus An evergreen, with glossy dark green leaves. It flowers throughout the winter with clusters of small white flowers with pink buds. 'Eve Price' is a good form with a more compact habit, smaller leaves and flowers tinged with pink. Zone 8

ESSENTIAL PERENNIALS, BIENNIALS AND ANNUALS

This group offers a huge range of plants, and the all-season plants among them make a diverse collection. Some have been selected for their double action of flowers and seedheads. This category includes allium, iris, lunaria and pulsatilla. Others qualify because, in addition to their flowers, they have especially worthwhile foliage. Among these are acanthus, alchemilla, hosta and silybum. Others again have been included because their display is so long-lived: among them are the hellebores and *Viola cornuta*. Substantial coverage is given to the ornamental grasses and sedges, a family of plants that is sometimes under-rated in gardens. The grasses have a subtle beauty that makes them irresistible to the discerning gardener. Moreover, as with most plants grown predominantly for their foliage, their peak season lasts much longer than the majority of floral displays. The same goes for ferns, for instance.

Most of the annuals and biennials featured here come under the heading of 'self-seeders'. Once established they will spring up all over the place, and will often produce more than one generation in a season. With self-seeders it is difficult to draw the line between asset and pest, but the best of them will bring distinction to your garden. Walls, steps and paths look all the better when clothed with an improvised display of plants that have arrived under their own steam. The effect is to soften the hard structural lines. By definition, of course, self-seeders can be left to their own devices. But they do not always appear in the right place. Gardening with these plants is not the usual active concern of growing seeds and planting out, but rather the passive business of rooting up self-sown seedlings that have sprung up where you do not want them.

The first mists of autumn have fallen, but still the annual *Cosmos* 'Sensation' is flowering at full strength. Young plants were put into the ground to replace tulips in early summer. The wispy fern-like foliage of the cosmos makes an unobtrusive companion to a sequence of border perennials. The cosmos comes into its own at midsummer and flowers continuously until mid-autumn, when the nights become too cold and the days too short for its buds to open. Then it is time to heave the plants out of the border and to replace them with bulbs, so that the cycle begins again for next year.

Acanthus spinosus seedheads

Acanthus spinosus

BEAR'S BREECHES

Architectural foliage, tall flower spikes
in late summer

Wherever it is placed in the garden, acanthus will create a powerful effect for much of the season, first by its dense and graceful foliage of shiny intense green, later by the sensational bicoloured flower spikes. Placed on its own in a prominent position it makes an attractive eye-catcher, but, by virtue of the subdued colours of its flowers, it is also a polite partner for other plants. It grows large, with arching leaves reaching a spread of 1.5m/5ft and the flowers towering to 1.8m/6ft. At this size you might assume that it only has a place in a large garden, but I would disagree. Even a garden that is little bigger than a pocket handkerchief does not have to be limited to miniature plants. Contrasts of scale are important in any planting, and in a small garden striking architectural perennials like acanthus can play a role equivalent to that of shrubs in a larger one. They are useful too if you want a labour-saving garden with fewer, larger plants.

Among the best of the acanthus is *Acanthus spinosus*. Its leaves are deeply divided and spiny, but though they look prickly they are perfectly soft and harmless. In shade the plant will produce only leaves, no flowers, but you would be perfectly justified in growing it solely for its foliage. It looks splendid in the company of hostas and ferns in a shady foliage garden.

A position in full sun will encourage the plant to flower. Held aloft on long, stiff stems, the flower spikes are as bold and prickly as the foliage is soft. The individual flowers are white, but they are hooded by an outer structure, the calyx, shaped like a mussel shell, of a distinctive silvery-green colour, tinged with purple. The base of each flower is fringed with stiff, thistle-like bracts, which make the flower head extremely prickly to handle. After the flowers have dropped, the spike, with its decorative calyces and bracts, survives well into the autumn while the seed containers swell to the size of marbles. Cut down at this stage, the spikes can be dried to join the vase of 'everlasting' flowers which extends the pleasure of your garden through the winter.

• Grow acanthus in full sun, in any well-drained soil. Split the plants after a few years, when they become overcrowded. Propagate by seed or by cuttings. Zone 7

ANOTHER ACANTHUS TO GROW

Acanthus mollis The leaves of *A. mollis* are not so deeply divided as those of *A. spinosus*. Otherwise it is very similar in appearance, and the harmless-looking flower heads have the same prickly bracts. It is a slightly less hardy plant, however. Zone 8

An appropriate setting, in front of a classical column, for a clump of *Acanthus mollis*. The Ancient Greeks used acanthus leaves as a *motif* in their architecture. Companion plants here include the thistle *Onopordum acanthium*, with acanthus-like leaves.

Agapanthus Headbourne Hybrids in late summer, with *Geranium psilostemon*

worth waiting for. And when it is finally time to cut down the seedheads they can easily be dried for the everlasting flower arrangement.

Agapanthus Headbourne Hybrids belong to the lily family and their flowers are not unlike those of another genus within the same family, the alliums or onions. The flower head is a globe of azure blue, made up of a mass of trumpet-shaped flowers on slender stalks radiating from the central stem.

Agapanthus is a native of South Africa, and even A. Headbourne Hybrids, hardiest of the clan, are only fully hardy in a warm climate. The need to protect the plants is one reason for growing agapanthus in pots, which you can put under cover for the winter. The plants also benefit from a relatively dry soil while they are dormant.

If you choose to grow agapanthus in the border, its blue flowers look well in association with yellow companions, especially the pale yellow of *Achillea* 'Moonshine' or *Anthemis tinctoria* 'E.C. Buxton'. For a

Agapanthus Headbourne Hybrids in autumn

Agapanthus Headbourne Hybrids

AFRICAN BLUE LILY

Globes of sky-blue flowers in late summer, autumn seedheads

It is possible to be *too* tidy in the garden. When the glorious blue flower heads of agapanthus begin to fade after several weeks of late summer display, it is tempting to cut them to the ground for the sake of tidiness. If you can resist this urge the plants will reward you with an autumn show of seedheads; more modest, I admit, than the summer flowers but still

cool effect, a background of silver foliage is striking; any of the artemisias will do. If your garden palette runs to bold colour relationships, then you might consider underplanting agapanthus with the lovely Californian fuchsia, *Zauschneria californica*. This produces a mass of pale red trumpets on silver-green foliage which will, with any luck, coincide with the flowers of your agapanthus.

• Height to 75cm/30in. Full sun, any soil. The strap-like leaves form clumps up to 60cm/24in wide, which die back in winter. Propagate by division of the roots in spring or autumn. Repot container-grown agapanthus every two or three years, splitting the plant each time to make sure it has room to expand. Agapanthus can be grown from seed, but will not reach flowering size for four years. Zone 8

OTHER AGAPANTHUS TO GROW

There are numerous varieties available, selected for size and for hue, and names are constantly changing. The hardiest types are those with narrow leaves that die back in winter. Plants with broad evergreen leaves are the least hardy, and need winter protection, but are among the most spectacular if you can protect them over winter.

Agapanthus campanulatus The ancestor of *A.* Headbourne Hybrids, similar in habit and size, with variable blue flowers ranging from powder-blue to ultramarine. There is an excellent white form, *A. campanulatus* var. *albidus*. Height 75cm/30in, spread 60cm/24in. Zone 8

Agapanthus 'Loch Hope' One of the best, but not commonly available. It is tall and sturdy, growing to a height of 1.2m/4ft with deep blue flowers that come late enough to coincide with early autumn performers such as sedums. Zone 8

Agrostemma githago
CORN COCKLE
Pink flowers throughout the summer

Agrostemma githago 'Milas' in summer, with phalaris

There was a time – before weedkillers and wall-to-wall farming – when cornfields were humming with wildlife. The corn was home to partridges and corn-crakes, rabbits and fieldmice, and a habitat for countless species of wild flowers. Among these was one that has now almost vanished from the fields – *Agrostemma githago*, the corn cockle.

One of the virtues of the corn cockle is that, in

our gardens as in the cornfields, it takes up very little space. The plant is adapted to surviving side by side with a tall-growing crop and so it should fit in with your existing planting without your having to make space for it.

The flowers, which are upward-facing and held on the tips of the plant, are wide open to the sun. The rims of the petals are dark pink, lightening to white towards the centre tube, and there are rays of dotted lines radiating inwards. They are pretty flowers, and look especially good in association with other flowers in the pink range, for instance the magenta *Geranium psilostemon* and old-fashioned roses, or else against a background of silver foliage, such as that of *Artemisia arborescens*.

The flowers last for several weeks but when they do begin to die off you are faced with a quandary. You will want to save seed for next year, and so the sensible course of action is to leave the seedheads to mature until the seeds are ready (after about six weeks). On the other hand, if you elect to dead-head the plants after flowering, you will have a second burst of flowers – but by the time they appear, up to two months later, it may be well into autumn, when it will be too late for seeds to mature. The best thing – as so often in gardening – is to compromise. Dead-head just half the plants within every clump for a second flowering and leave the remaining seedheads to mature.

• Grows to 90cm/36in high. Any soil, full sun or part-shade. Plant seeds in places where you wish the plants to flower, staggering sowings over several weeks to make sure that germination takes place and also to extend the flowering season. If the plants are not supported by their neighbours they will need a few twigs to hold them up. The most commonly available seed is *Agrostemma githago* 'Milas', which is almost identical to the wild form but a little more vigorous. Grow as an annual.

Alchemilla mollis

LADY'S MANTLE

Long-lived lime-green flower sprays above soft scalloped foliage

Alchemilla is the perfect foil. Almost any other plant looks well against its sprays of lime-green flowers and soft, velvety leaves. Used at the edge of a border it makes a gentle frame to the garden picture. It tumbles attractively from raised beds and across paths and steps, softening the hard lines of the garden wherever it falls.

And few plants are so easy to use. It is adaptable to any soil and any prospect, sun or shade. In short, it is a near-perfect gardener's friend and its only disadvantage could be that it is so widely used that it may have become something of a cliché. My philosophy, however, is totally to ignore fashion in one's choice of plants. If you like a plant, whether it is common or not, use it.

The young clumps of tiny flowers stand proud of the leaves but they soon begin to slump and sprawl. Nobody would accuse this of being a tidy plant. Its relaxed habit makes it a useful element in the romantic garden, where it looks good as an underplanting to heavy swags of old-fashioned roses.

Although the flowers look presentable for at least a month in summer, they do begin to turn brown sooner or later. At this stage you can cut back the whole plant, leaves and all, down to the base. This encourages it to put on new growth. Fresh young leaves soon appear and it will throw up a further burst of flowers in early autumn. The cut flowers can be dried for the winter.

The leaves make a dense and attractive ground cover. Scallop-shaped, they are as soft to the touch as blotting paper, yet totally unabsorbent. It is one of this plant's most endearing properties that drops of rainwater or dew collect in hollows in the leaves and remain there until the sun dries them off.

RIGHT The lime-green flowers of *Alchemilla mollis* provide a good foil for almost any other colour.

FAR RIGHT Despite being so soft, the leaves of *Alchemilla mollis* are impervious to water. Rainwater collects on the surface in drops like beads of mercury.

• Height 45cm/18in, spread 60cm/24in. Propagate by division of the dense root clump in autumn or spring. The plant will also seed itself, often finding its way to cracks between stones on paths and terraces. Zone 3

ANOTHER ALCHEMILLA TO GROW

Alchemilla conjuncta A more compact and tidier version of *A. mollis.* Again the flowers are lime-green, but they are held in smaller, tighter inflorescences. The leaves are more brittle-looking, star-shaped in outline with their edges defined by a line of tiny white hairs. A useful plant for the rock garden, to accompany miniature bulbs and alpines. Height 20cm/8in, spread 30cm/12in. Zone 4

Allium christophii in summer

Allium christophii
Lilac-coloured flowers in early summer,
everlasting seedheads

No garden, however small, is complete without bulbs; every gardener loves tulips, narcissi, lilies and their friends and relations and will find space for them. Sadly, though, most bulbs are unquestionably single-season plants. Their performance has only one act – sensational perhaps in its time but usually of brief duration. When their flowers are finished there is not much supporting show from the leaves. But there is an exception among bulbous plants, one that produces spectacular flower heads that can be dried and kept for ever. This is *Allium christophii* (syn.

Allium christophii in autumn

A. albopilosum), a member of the onion family, as you will recognize from the smell if you accidentally cut into its bulb. The flower heads of *A. christophii* are among the most exotic in the summer garden. Each head is made up of star-shaped, lilac-coloured flowers arranged around the circumference of a globe and supported by stalks radiating like spokes from the centre. They might remind you of one of those fireworks that shatters into trails of light, each line terminating in its own star-like burst.

Unlike a firework, however, this allium flower goes on and on. For up to a month the flower head keeps its colour, and when it fades it retains its lovely structure. It dries on the stem so that its intricate skeleton remains in place, with round black seeds developing in threes in the eye of each flower. These dried seedheads look striking in the border, but sadly they are very brittle and easily damaged by wind and rain. I think that you would do best to pick them from the base and keep them inside, where they will last for ever. I admit, however, that I love them so much that when in late summer I come to show a guest around the garden, I go beforehand and gently push a few of the stems back into the ground to make a temporary clump.

When deliberating where to plant this allium, you might bear in mind that its structure, rather than its colour, is its most striking feature. Regard it as an architectural plant and use it in clumps as an eye-catcher at the corners of beds and similar strategic points. It looks good in silhouette against the dark background of yew or box. If you can associate it with plants whose colour will complement that of the allium flower, so much the better. I think that its rather subdued lilac colour could do with a lift and would suggest placing it with colours from the opposite side of the spectrum, the yellows for example. It would look good growing through the yellow-leaved ground-covering creeping jenny, *Lysimachia nummularia* 'Aurea', and backed by a golden

shrub such as *Philadelphus coronarius* 'Aureus' or the yellow privet, *Ligustrum ovalifolium* 'Aureum'. A clever idea would be to underplant it with yellow-flowered *Allium moly*, which grows to a height of 25cm/10in and flowers at the same time.

● Height 60cm/24in, spread minimal, but allow 30cm/12in for the foliage. The flower heads are up to 23cm/9in in diameter. Plant the bulbs in autumn. For growing in clumps, place them 15cm/6in apart, and about 8cm/3in below the surface. Full sun is preferable but they are tolerant of any soil. Feed the leaves with foliar feed to sustain the bulbs so that they will flower again the following year. Zone 4

OTHER ALLIUMS TO GROW

Once you have grown one type of allium you are likely to become addicted and will want to grow more. There is a wide range available, with a huge diversity of flower colour, form, height and season. They are among the most rewarding groups of plants.

Allium aflatunense Spheres of pinky-lilac star-shaped flowers 10cm/4in across are held high above the foliage on stems of 90cm/36in. It flowers in late spring, and looks sensational in mass plantings, as at Barnsley House in Gloucestershire where it is used as an underplanting along the laburnum walk. The flower heads keep well when dry. Zone 4

Allium cernuum In summer the deep rose-pink flowers hang gracefully from loose flower heads about 40cm/15in above the ground. Full sun and dry conditions. Zone 3

Allium sphaerocephalon Flowers in late summer, with compact burgundy flower heads about 60cm/24in high. Zone 6

Allium sphaerocephalon

Allium cernuum

Allium moly

Arum italicum pictum

LORDS AND LADIES

Striking foliage, creamy-yellow spring flowers,
red berries in autumn and winter

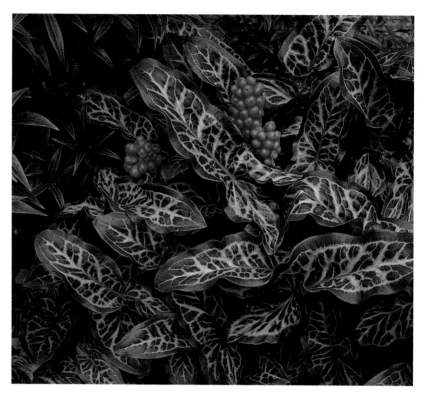

The hardy arums are among the earliest foliage plants to show themselves in spring. The first young leaves, furled up in tight cylinders like umbrellas, may appear above the last of the winter snows and in spite of their delicate appearance they survive all but the hardest frosts. There are about sixteen species of arum, not all of them hardy, and they all have beautiful arrow-shaped leaves. In several varieties this foliage is enhanced by patterns of variegation and perhaps the best among these is *Arum italicum pictum* (syn. *A. italicum* ssp. *italicum*). This form has narrow dark green leaves with a network of veins picked out in white. These striking leaves make a bold accompaniment to the earliest spring bulbs such as snowdrops, crocus and scillas, some of which have rather modest foliage of their own. The arum leaves look good, too, with the young growth of many of the smaller grasses, such as *Milium effusum* 'Aureum'.

If you are lucky, your arums will flower for you in spring. The flowers are creamy-yellow spathes, hooded like a monk's cowl, but they are unostentatious and you may need to stoop down and grope among the foliage to see them. In summer, as the leaves die back, the seed spike is left standing with shiny green berries developing along its length. By autumn the berries have coloured to vivid scarlet and soon they are joined by the first of the new leaves. So here is a plant of almost continuous interest, with something to offer in every season.

• Height to 40cm/15in, with clumps spreading to 60cm/24in. Any soil but prefers plenty of moisture, provided that drainage is good. Part-shade or full sun. Arums survive underground as tubers: propagate by splitting congested clumps. Zone 6

OTHER ARUMS TO GROW

Arum italicum pictum in late winter

Zantedeschia aethiopica The arum lilies are a separate genus from the arums, but they belong together in the same family, the Araceae or aroids. Grown for their wonderful funnel-shaped white flowers, the arum lilies have dark green leaves, arrow-shaped like those of the arums, but on a much larger scale. Clumps of *Zantedeschia aethiopica* reach 1.2m/4ft height and 90cm/36in spread. They are not hardy in any but the mildest sites and in most areas it is best to consider them as conservatory plants. They like full sun and plenty of moisture – they can be grown as aquatics with their feet in water. Among the best varieties are *Z. aethiopica* 'Crowborough' with pure white spathes, and *Z. aethiopica* 'Green Goddess', in which the spathes have broad green lips and margins. Zone 8/9

Beta vulgaris

RUBY CHARD

Long-lasting red stems below dense green foliage

Here is a vegetable that deserves promotion from the kitchen garden to the ornamental border. Closely related to perpetual spinach and Swiss chard, it has stems like those of rhubarb, but more intensely red.

Ruby chard will contribute an exciting flash of scarlet to a mixed border, and is an obvious choice as an ingredient of an all-red border. Here it can be associated with perennials and annuals with red flowers to give an illusion that flowers and stems are part of the same plant.

• Stems up to 45cm/18in long. Ruby chard is simple to grow from seed sown directly in the ground in spring. Any soil, sun or part-shade. Grow as an annual.

Beta vulgaris in summer, with red *Nicotiana alata*

Brassica oleracea

ORNAMENTAL CABBAGE

Colourful foliage, maintained over a long season

A plant that invites a lot of interest in my garden in the late season is only a cabbage – a selected form of the common cabbage, grown as an annual for its attractive variegated foliage. I like to grow it in clumps of two or three in the herbaceous border, where it is so unexpected that many visitors ask what it can be.

There are two colour forms of this plant, purple and cream. Evidently they cannot be separated by breeding as they appear in more or less equal numbers from each packet of seeds. Fortunately the colour bias is already evident in young plants even before the pattern of variegation has developed. You can discern a tinge of pink in the leaf bases of plants that are going to be purple; those of the cream plants are clear green. It is useful to know which is which when you place the young plants in the border, so that they will associate well with their neighbours.

The cream version looks effective in a white border, with white companions such as Shasta daisies, annual sweet peas and *Dimorphotheca pluvialis* 'Glistening White'. I like to place the purple form in the border among blue penstemons and *Aster* × *frikartii*, whose purple-blue flowers pick up an echo in the intense, shiny purple of the cabbage. Unlike most plants in the border, the ornamental cabbage improves with the onset of winter. The first frosts intensify the coloration of the plant. With a sparkling layer of frost the cabbage looks like some deep-frozen delicacy of *nouvelle cuisine*. It can survive a hard winter, but when it begins to look tatty in early spring it is doomed, I am afraid, for the compost heap. Then it is time to grow new plants from seed.

• Height and spread 40cm/15in. Any soil, sun or part-shade. Grow as an annual.

Brassica oleracea 'White Peacock' in summer, in a white and cream planting

Brassica oleracea in winter

Campanula portenschlagiana
Profuse blue flowers in summer

If you can establish *Campanula portenschlagiana* (syn. *C. muralis*) in a crack between the stones of a terrace, with any luck it will spread by runners between the stones so that eventually you have a network of low-growing blue flowers for midsummer. Provided that it has full sun, this campanula is a great colonizer of inhospitable corners.

The violet-blue flowers are bell-shaped, which is typical of the genus. They grow so densely on the plant that you can scarcely see the leaves when it is in bloom. For the rest of the summer the leaves, which are small and scallop-shaped, make a mound of some 40cm/15in height and spread.

A closely related species is *C. poscharskyana*. This has flowers with narrower petals, so that they look star-shaped; they are a more subtle, washed-out lilac. It is another colonizer of gaps in stone paths and it will take root in a dry-stone wall and climb some way up. This makes it a useful underplanting for wall shrubs, provided that the sun can reach it.

For ground cover on a larger scale, you might also consider the tall perennial *C. persicifolia*, which reaches a height of 90cm/36in, comes in blue, lilac or white varieties and spreads itself by seed.

● *C. portenschlagiana* and *C. poscharskyana* thrive on benign neglect. *C. persicifolia* is happy in sun or part-shade, any soil. *C. portenschlagiana* is hardy to zone 5, *C. poscharskyana* to zone 3, *C. persicifolia* to zone 4.

Campanula poscharskyana
in summer

Filling in the cracks.
Campanula portenschlagiana
colonizes a stone path
where few other plants
would survive. The path
bakes in the sun, but the
campanula's roots reach
under the stones to find
moisture.

Centranthus ruber

VALERIAN

Flowers from summer to autumn

Valerian is a survivor. You will see it on waste land and in derelict gardens where it competes successfully with encroaching weeds, unlike the more refined garden plants which disappear as soon as they have to fend for themselves. Valerian will seed itself in the most unlikely places, and you will see it growing high above the ground from cracks in the mortar on buildings and on garden walls. Don't dismiss it as a weed, though, just because it behaves like one. Valerian is a beautiful and useful garden plant, with an exceptionally long flowering period. Butterflies and other insects find the deep pink flower heads irresistible.

Valerian looks well when grown in clumps in the herbaceous border. The pure white form is even more useful in this context, as it may be easier to associate with the other occupants of the border. Another way to grow this perennial is to encourage it to seed in the cracks between stones on a terrace or wall. Here, like other colonizers, it will soften the hard lines of the garden architecture, and give your garden a lived-in look.

• Height and spread 90cm/36in. Any soil, even poor ground, chalk, limestone or rubble, where few other garden plants will survive. Does best in full sun. Propagate by seed. Zone 5

Pink, red and white seedlings of valerian *(Centranthus ruber)* have taken root under the iron railings of a small cottage garden, contributing to a cheerful riot of colour. Beyond, a smoke bush, *Cotinus coggygria* 'Royal Purple', is just coming into flower. Its dark and sombre tone provides a good foil for the brilliant colours around it. Behind it against the wall is the climbing version of the curious bicoloured rose 'Masquerade'.

Cornus canadensis flowers

Cornus canadensis

CREEPING DOGWOOD

Foliage for ground cover, white flowers in summer, followed by red berries

It comes as something of a surprise to find that this useful ground-cover perennial is a relation of the dogwood trees and shrubs (pages 28–9, 64–6), but if you look carefully at its flowers and leaves you will see that they are similar in structure to those of the more familiar dogwoods. The flowers, which appear in midsummer, are pure white and about 2.5cm/1in across. They consist of broad, flat white bracts surrounding small flower parts of green and purple. In autumn the plant bears clusters of red berries. The leaves are mid-green and oval and grow in whorls at the tips of the spreading shoots.

● Height 15cm/6in, spread 60cm/24in. Requires acid soil and is suited to peat beds and acidic woodland conditions in shade or part-shade. Zone 2

Corydalis lutea

Ferny foliage, yellow flowers from spring right through the summer

Once you have *Corydalis lutea* (syn. *Pseudofumaria lutea*) in the garden you are unlikely ever to be without it again. Some would call this a mixed blessing but, as with most other self-seeders, if you keep this plant under control it will be a tremendous asset. It will appear and survive in the most unlikely places, where few other plants will find a hold. In particular, it will colonize old walls and paths and establish lush growth in the smallest gaps between the stones, somehow finding moisture in places where you would have thought there was none. Its effect is to soften the hard edges of a garden, like a curtain softening the line of a window.

The foliage is blue-green and frilly, like that of one of the more delicate ferns. The flowers appear from spring right through the summer. They are little yellow down-turned tubes, growing together in short inflorescences just above the foliage.

Corydalis ochroleuca (syn. *Pseudofumaria alba*) has cream-coloured flowers but is identical to *C. lutea* in all other respects. Many gardeners find it even more desirable, as the cream flowers are perhaps easier to associate with other plants.

● Corydalis makes a gently rounded mound up to 40cm/15in in height and spread. A plant that thrives on neglect, it will make its own way around your garden, seeding as it goes and surviving in dry, poor soil and sun or shade. The only cultivation necessary is to pull it up by the roots in places where it is unwelcome. Zone 5

Corydalis lutea, self-seeded in a wall

Cosmos 'Sensation'

Feathery foliage, flowers from midsummer
through to autumn

The majority of annuals selected for this book are self-seeders that, once established, will appear every year without any effort on the part of the gardener. Cosmos and other tender annuals only self-seed in frost-free climates; elsewhere, they are used as bedding plants. Cosmos is the only bedding plant that I have included here, selecting it for its exceptionally long flowering period and the additional attraction of its fine feathery foliage. It is a rather controversial choice, I admit, because there are so many other worthy bedding plants that deserve a spare in every garden, so might claim one in this book. What about the tobacco plant, *Nicotiana alata* (syn. *N. affinis*), with an equally long flowering period and a divine scent, or the annual rudbeckias that light up the summer and autumn border? I am also tempted by the exotic *Cleome hassleriana* (syn. *C. spinosa*) and the magnificent foliage plant *Ricinus communis.* But this cosmos will have to stand for all of them.

Cosmos 'Sensation' is a robust plant, but not at all bulky, as its delicate fern-like foliage permits you to see through to the plants beyond. This attractive framework is covered with flowers from midsummer right through to the first frosts of autumn. The flowers are like broad-petalled daisies in shape, in shades of dark pink, magenta and white, with golden-yellow centres. As with other annuals, it is important to dead-head the plant to encourage it to continue flowering. The flowering stems of cosmos have a branching structure that makes dead-heading easy. Each mature flower has two budding stems which branch off at the base of its stalk. To remove the dead head, you simply cut the stalk at the branching point and one flower is replaced by two. When these two are over, you cut their joint stem lower down, at the point at which two further

branches arise. Aided by dead-heading, multiplication of flowers continues through the summer.

The magenta and pink tones of the cosmos flowers harmonize well in the summer-to-autumn border with verbenas, penstemons and perennial asters selected within the range of pink through purple. I find that the cosmos also makes a striking contrast with yellow foliage; it looks marvellous as an underplanting to a yellow-leaved tree such as *Robinia pseudoacacia* 'Frisia'.

• Height 1.2m/4ft, spread 75cm/30in. Sow seed under glass in spring, and prick out into larger pots, as with other tender annuals. Harden the plants off gradually. Do not plant out until all risk of late frosts has passed. This time usually coincides with periods at which it is safe to remove the foliage of spring bulbs and, whether or not you lift the bulbs, the cosmos and other annuals may be planted out to take their place. Cosmos will thrive in any soil but it needs full sun. Grow as an annual.

Cosmos 'Sensation' in summer

Crambe maritima in summer

Crambe maritima

SEA KALE

Young growth used as a vegetable, silvery-grey
foliage, white flowers in summer

Sea kale is equally at home in the border or the
vegetable plot, but you have to decide at the outset
whether to grow it to eat or for its ornamental effect.
If you pick the young growth for the pot you will
have a delicious vegetable, but the summer display
will be much reduced. I favour planting it in the
border, where it makes a mound of curly leaves, not
unlike true kale but silvery in colour. In midsummer
the plant is crowned by dense sprays of small white
flowers.

• A perennial of height 60cm/24in, spread
1.2m/4ft. Happy in any soil, prefers full sun. Propagate by seed or by division. Zone 6

ANOTHER CRAMBE TO GROW

Crambe cordifolia One of the most dramatic of all
architectural plants, *C. cordifolia* produces a haze of
sweet-scented white flowers on stems up to 2m/7ft
tall at midsummer. The plant makes a romantic
accompaniment to old-fashioned roses and delphiniums. However, it has a long lead-up time to its
brief moment of glory, and it produces large dark
green leaves which take up a lot of space in the
border and are irresistible to slugs. Zone 6

Cyclamen hederifolium

Autumn flowers, decorative winter and spring foliage

There can be few more cheering sights in the woodland garden than that of the first flowers of *Cyclamen hederifolium* (formerly known as *C. neapolitanum*) peeping bare-headed from the dark soil in early autumn. These woodland beauties are far smaller and more delicate in proportion than the cyclamen hybrids that we give and receive as house plants. Their little shuttlecock heads are only about 1cm/½in long and stand a mere 8cm/3in above the ground. But what they lack in stature they make up – once established – in quantity. A mature colony in ideal conditions can cover a large area, within which the ground will be overlaid for several autumn weeks

Cyclamen hederifolium in autumn

Cyclamen hederifolium in winter

with a carpet of flowers. But there is no need to aspire to this scale of display. You can enjoy this plant in the smallest garden, provided that you can reproduce the conditions that it favours. It will need an undisturbed site, in shade, and an annual top-dressing of leaf mould, corresponding to the natural covering of leaves that it would receive in its woodland habitat.

One of the charms of this species is the variability of both flowers and leaves. At the two extremes the flowers may be pure white or dark mauve, but they are most commonly somewhere between the two, in a shade of pale pink. This cyclamen is appropriately named *hederifolium*, which means 'ivy-leaved'. The leaf is reminiscent of the ivy not only in its shape, but also in its extraordinary variability of pattern. No two plants seem to have the same leaves. Some are dark green, marked with patterns of a paler tone. Others are overlaid with bold dashes of silver like the brushstrokes of an expressionist painter. Others again are silver all over. The underside, however, is always a deep red. It is a lovely feature of this plant that the leaves usually emerge after the flowers have appeared but before they have died down, so both are present together for some of the time. The foliage survives through the winter and well into spring, to give an attractive ground cover at a time when there is not much other greenery on the woodland floor.

The cyclamen survives from year to year as a corm, just below the surface of the soil. The corm is flattish and grows up to the diameter of a saucer: a corm of mature size will give up to fifty flowers at a time, growing from little knobs on the top surface. A curiosity of the plant is that the roots appear from the top surface of the corm, so it is easy to make the mistake of planting the cyclamen upside down. The safest thing is to buy the plants in flower, in pots, and transplant them gently into your garden. This way you can be certain that they are the right way up.

• Requires a shady site, as described above, and a shallow mulch in summer of compost or leaf mould to cover the corm. The plant will spread by seeding itself, but you can help it along by spreading the seed. The seedheads mature in late spring, at the tip of the coiled stalks. When they are ripe, collect the seeds and dab them directly into the soil. Zone 5

ANOTHER CYCLAMEN TO GROW

Cyclamen coum An early spring beauty on the same scale as *C. hederifolium*, and in a similar range of colouring. Typically the flowers are fuchsia-pink, on a relatively short stem, and the leaves are variably patterned with silver on the upper surface, and crimson on the underside. Zone 7

Cynara cardunculus

CARDOON

Silver foliage from spring to autumn, blue summer flowers that can be dried for winter display

A close relation to the globe artichoke, the cardoon is one of the best silver foliage plants, if you have space in the borders to accommodate its bulky spread of 1.8m/6ft. Its young growth, in spring, looks wonderful underplanted with black tulips, such as *Tulipa* 'Queen of Night', or *T.* 'Black Parrot'. It also combines effectively with silver-leaved *Artemisia* 'Powis Castle' and purple-leaved sage. Its long leaves, coming from the centre, soft and deeply cut, are enough for it to qualify as an outstanding plant, but as a bonus it offers summer flowers like huge deep blue thistle-heads, perched some 2.5m/8ft above the ground. The flowers can be picked and dried for winter.

• Any soil, full sun. Propagate by seed or by division in the spring. Not fully hardy in cold, damp areas, where it is prudent to cover it in winter. Zone 8

Centrepiece of a silver garden, a superb specimen of the cardoon, *Cynara cardunculus.* At its feet are the silver grass, *Festuca glauca,* and lamb's ears, *Stachys byzantina.* Behind is one of the best silver-leaved shrubs, *Elaeagnus angustifolia* 'Caspica'. White-flowered phlox and blue delphiniums add an appropriate touch of cool colour to the silver harmonies of this border. It makes sense to grow silver-foliage plants together as, with a few exceptions, they tend to flourish in similar conditions. All the plants in this picture prefer full sun in summer and resent becoming waterlogged in cold winter weather.

Dicentra formosa 'Stuart Boothman' in late spring

Dicentra spectabilis in early summer, with forget-me-nots

Dicentra formosa 'Stuart Boothman'

Grey-green foliage, pink flowers in late spring
and early summer

The dicentras are invaluable foliage plants with the additional virtue of attractive flowers. One of the very best of them is *Dicentra formosa* 'Stuart Boothman', in which the subdued mid-pink flowers provide a perfect complement to the finely cut grey-green leaves. This fern-like foliage looks particularly well in shady corners with ferns and hostas. The long-lasting heart-shaped flowers hang on short arching stems just above the leaves.

• Makes a mound of height and spread 45cm/18in in any humus-rich soil. Thrives in shade or part-shade. Zone 5

ANOTHER DICENTRA TO GROW

Dicentra spectabilis The ever-popular 'bleeding heart' grows much taller, to a height and spread of 75cm/30in, with rather coarse foliage but with intriguing heart-shaped pink flowers, tipped with white. The flowers last over many weeks in early summer. There is also a beautiful pure white form, *D. spectabilis alba*. Zone 3

Erigeron karvinskianus

White and pale pink flowers from spring to autumn

Consider the daisies in your lawn. Lawn daisies keep flowering from early spring to late autumn and they spread themselves unremittingly in the meantime. If only they grew in the right place they might be regarded as valuable plants. Fortunately, they have a family relation which has all their positive qualities, but is much less invasive. This is a low-growing perennial daisy from Mexico called *Erigeron karvinskianus* (syn. *E. mucronatus*).

At first sight the flowers of this daisy are identical to those of the lawn weed. The same size, about 1cm/½in across, they are white with a golden eye. However, as they age the flowers take on a pale pink tinge and this gives the plant a special two-tone attraction when there are young and old flowers together. The flowers keep coming the whole summer long. The foliage of this erigeron is much more attractive than that of the lawn daisy: its leaves are lance-shaped and their habit is more upright.

The erigeron is equally at home in a rock garden or tumbling down between the stones of a dry-stone wall, and it looks marvellous growing in the cracks between the stones on a patio or terrace. It seeds itself prodigiously, but it is so pretty that you will probably be delighted when it pops up in unexpected places. If it arrives in the wrong place you can simply pull it up by the roots (it will not survive in a lawn).

• Height 23cm/9in, spread 40cm/15in. Prefers sun, but is happy in any soil. Propagate by division or allow it to seed itself. Hardy to zone 9; grow as an annual elsewhere.

Cascading down a low wall, a mound of *Erigeron karvinskianus* makes a fluid outline at the edge of a flight of steps. In this position, in full sun, the daisy ought to flower for most of the summer and will seed itself further in cracks between the stones of the wall.

Eryngium alpinum in summer, with erigerons

Eryngium alpinum

ALPINE SEA HOLLY

Blue-green foliage, long-lasting blue summer flowers

If you scrutinize a single flower of *Eryngium alpinum* it might remind you of one of those seventeenth-century Dutch portraits of a solemn burgher of Amsterdam, his oval head rising from the most monumental ruff, and the whole effect tinted overall with a blue haze. Add together the dozen or more heads produced by a single plant and you have an astonishing picture.

Eryngium alpinum is probably the most striking member of a dramatic genus, the sea hollies. It is thistle-like in its upright habit and in the dry prickliness of its parts. As the flowers mature, the whole of the upper part of the plant becomes suffused with blue. This blue tinge extends throughout the stems to the knobbly cones of the flower heads and to the surrounding fringe or 'ruff' of bracts. It is these bracts that give this plant its distinction. They are smooth and metallic in texture, with cut, spiny edges like the finest filigree silverwork. Lower down on the plant the leaves are similarly patterned but less emphatically. They are dark blue-green veined with white, deeply divided and quite prickly along the edges.

In the border the drama of this plant would be heightened by partnering it with plants of contrasting textures and colours. I would venture to try it with one of the verbascums with woolly grey leaves, such as *Verbascum olympicum*. Not only would

Eryngium × oliverianum in summer

the leaves provide an effective contrast, but the pale yellow flower spikes of the verbascum would complement the blue of the eryngium. Another idea would be to back the eryngium with a mound of yellow grass: *Hakonechloa macra* 'Aureola' or *Carex elata* 'Aurea'.

Alive in the border the plant already looks like a dried flower, with a seemingly artificial spray-coat of blue. Removed, it dries readily to join the arrangement of everlasting flowers in the jug on the mantelpiece for winter.

● Height 90cm/36in, spread 60cm/24in. Needs full sun but will survive in any soil, including poor, stony soils, and even on gravel paths. *E. alpinum* is a perennial that can be propagated by division, from root cuttings, or from seed. Zone 4

OTHER ERYNGIUMS TO GROW

Eryngium bourgatii A relatively delicate plant with numerous small globular flower heads fringed with spiky bracts. The flower heads take on a lilac-blue tinge as they mature. For attractive flower colour it is important to choose a good form, such as *E. bourgatii* 'Oxford Blue'. Height 60cm/24in, spread 45cm/18in. Zone 5

Eryngium giganteum Known as 'Miss Willmott's ghost' (see page 12), this biennial dies after flowering but will readily seed itself. Growing to a height of 1.2m/4ft and spread of 75cm/30in, it has striking flower heads with broad, silvery bracts. Zone 4

Eryngium × oliverianum Another blue-headed sea holly, not unlike *E. alpinum*, which may well be one of its ancestors. It grows to a height of 90cm/36in and spread of 60cm/24in and the flowers, stems and bracts are a steely lilac-blue. The bracts are less intricately cut than in *E. alpinum*. Zone 4

Eryngium giganteum, with evening primróse and pink phlox

Erysimum 'Bowles' Mauve'

Evergreen foliage, mauve flowers all year round

The perennial wallflower *Erysimum* 'Bowles' Mauve' is included here by virtue of its almost constant performance all the year round. The more familiar biennial wallflowers, in any colour between sulphur-yellow and deep crimson, flower for up to six weeks in early summer. 'Bowles' Mauve', however, can be almost guaranteed to flower in every month of the year, unless the winter is especially harsh (in which case the plant may be wiped out, as it is not reliably hardy). It is evergreen and its dark grey-blue leaves make an attractive combination with its flower heads, which are a delicate shade of mauve.

Its very vigour is its undoing. Within a year it makes a mound up to 1m/39in high, covered in flower spikes. But it is woody and brittle and tends to look leggy. It is best to take a few cuttings and grow fresh plants at least every other year.

There are other perennial wallflowers available, in a range of colours. One of the best is *E.* 'Moonlight', a hybrid of height 30cm/12in, with yellow flowers.

● Height and spread up to 1m/39in. Full sun, any soil (like other wallflowers it thrives in poor soil). Propagate by cuttings. Zone 8

Erysimum 'Bowles' Mauve'

Euphorbia characias wulfenii

Blue-green foliage, lime-green flower heads
from late spring into summer

I have found that the more obsessed you become with gardening, the more you begin to appreciate the relatively modest-looking plants that would not earn a second glance from a non-gardener. Here is a case in point. When a friend gave me a seedling of *Euphorbia characias* ssp. *wulfenii* some years ago I rather grudgingly allowed it space in the border to avoid hurting his feelings. Now, several years on, I would say that this single plant has given me more continuing pleasure than any other in the garden.

It is a plant that never looks unsightly. It matures elegantly through the autumn and winter, and then flowers for a lengthy period from late spring into summer. It is graceful even in decline. And yet, in colour at least, it is a discreet plant; never dominant, but a well-mannered foil for the more colourful flowers around it.

In full flower it is a symphony of greens. The leaf fronds are grey-green. Fanning out from a narrow base, they are surmounted by mop-like flower heads, which are lime-green. The flowers themselves are tiny and are enclosed within rounded bracts rather as a candle sits within a wall sconce. It is these bracts that give the flower head its overall lime-green colour. They are also the secret of the flower head's long life. As each little flower passes through its life cycle – from bud, through the fertile stage when it

Two phases in the long-lasting performance of *Euphorbia characias* ssp. *wulfenii*. In this border the euphorbia is already in action when narcissi come into flower in early spring, but it is at its peak to coincide with tulips a few weeks later. Later still, in midsummer, when *Geranium × magnificum* and white marguerites are in flower around its base, the euphorbia flowers are still presentable, though the seeds are now forming.

121

Euphorbia myrsinites in spring, with *Muscari armeniacum*

sports bright yellow stamens, to its final globular seeds – all this time the surrounding bract hardly changes. Between twelve and sixteen weeks the bracts hold out, only becoming a little more brittle and colouring to bronze as time wears on. Picked, the flower head dries well. Even without their flower heads, the remaining leaf fronds look attractive. And beneath their skirts next year's growth has already begun. Miniature fronds are growing up from the base, to take the place of the spent stems.

• Being a plant of Mediterranean origin, this euphorbia requires full sun but is content with poor soil, even growing from gaps between stones in a path. Zone 8

OTHER EUPHORBIAS TO GROW

Euphorbia characias Identical to *E. characias* ssp. *wulfenii* in size and shape, but has a tiny black eye to the individual flowers. Zone 8

***Euphorbia amygdaloides* 'Purpurea'** A euphorbia for shade, but rather susceptible to mildew in dry conditions. The pointed leaves are a lovely tint of green tinged with purple. It has khaki-coloured flower heads in early summer. Height to 60cm/24in. *E. amygdaloides* var. *robbiae* is a more vigorous plant, with dark green leaves in rosettes and loose heads of lime-green flowers. Zone 8

Euphorbia cyparissias An attractive but invasive low-growing euphorbia, up to 30cm/12in in height. It has wispy grey-green foliage and small lime-green flower heads in late spring. It spreads by runners under the soil and can be difficult to eliminate if it gets out of hand. Zone 3

Euphorbia myrsinites A lovely sprawling spurge, suitable for the rock garden or raised bed, where its stems can hang over the side. They are covered with stiff blue-green leaves and tipped with long-lasting lime-green flower heads. Looks especially good with blue spring bulbs such as scilla or muscari. Zone 5

Euphorbia polychroma A marvellous accompaniment to spring bulbs, this euphorbia makes a mound about 45cm/18in high and 60cm/24in in diameter, covered with bright yellow flower heads. Zone 4

Euphorbia polychroma in spring, with forget-me-nots

Geranium psilostemon

Long-lived magenta flowers in summer, finely cut leaves, colouring in autumn

No garden would be complete without its quota of hardy geraniums (or cranesbills). Most of them will contribute to a plant combination without becoming dominant or overbearing. Their flowers are refreshingly simple in shape and come in a range of clear colours, from whites through pinks and blues to mauves, magentas and purples. Most flower over quite a long season, and when they are over they die gracefully. When the flower petals have dropped the deeply cut foliage provides further interest for the rest of the season, and in some cases the leaves colour up well in autumn.

Another advantage of geraniums is that they come in sizes to suit any garden, from tiny alpine species to the magnificent *Geranium psilostemon*, which reaches a height of 1.5m/5ft and spread of 2m/7ft. This geranium has flowers of the most exotic colour – a vivid magenta veined with black and with a black centre. The leaves are exotic too, fan-shaped and deeply cut. They turn to shades of red and yellow in autumn. Some gardeners find it difficult to place this geranium as its colour is so intense. But it harmonizes well with old-fashioned roses in the deep pink to purple range, such as *Rosa* 'Madame Isaac Pereire' or *R.* 'Cardinal de Richelieu'. It also makes a striking contrast with grey-leaved plants such as artemisias, and looks good with blues. With reds and yellows, however, the contrasts are just too strong for comfort.

- Flourishes in any soil. Sun or part-shade. In an open border it will need staking, but if it is beside roses or other shrubs it will find its own support by sprawling among them. Propagate by division or by seed – you will often find self-sown seedlings around the base of the plant. Zone 4

OTHER GERANIUMS TO GROW

Geranium endressii An evergreen geranium, with a very long flowering season. The silvery-pink flowers appear throughout the summer and there are usually a few to be seen during mild spells through the winter. It seeds itself readily and makes good ground cover, especially under roses. The variety 'Wargrave Pink' has prolific salmon-pink flowers. Height 45cm/18in, spread 75cm/30in. Zone 4

Geranium 'Johnson's Blue' A deservedly popular blue geranium. Clumps reach a height of 45cm/18in and a spread of 60cm/24in. I have seen it planted impressively *en masse* along a winding gravel path. All traces of the leaves disappear in winter. Zone 4

Geranium × magnificum One of the larger geraniums, making a clump of height 60cm/24in and spread 1.2m/4ft. The flowers are deep violet, with

An effective partnership between *Geranium psilostemon* and an old-fashioned rose. Not only do their colours harmonize, but also the geranium can use the rose as a support.

OPPOSITE Old-fashioned roses underplanted with *Geranium endressii.* The geranium has spread to fill all the available ground space, suppressing weeds and covering the bare stems of the roses. The rose in front supports a tall *Geranium psilostemon.*

BELOW A border containing plants in the blue to purple range, contrasting with yellows and creams. Central at the front, *Geranium* 'Johnson's Blue' is framed by the yellow flower heads of *Allium moly* and variegated astrantia.

darker veins, and the leaves are rounded and deeply cut. It looks good with yellow or lime-green partners, such as *Achillea* 'Moonshine', or any of the euphorbias. Unfortunately, the flowering period of *G. × magnificum* is relatively short – just a few weeks – and its bulk may put off some gardeners. There is another dark violet geranium which would be an excellent substitute. This is *G. clarkei* 'Kashmir Purple', which reaches a height of 50cm/20in and spread of 75cm/30in, and flowers over a long period in summer. There is also a good white variety, *G. clarkei* 'Kashmir White'. Zone 4

Geranium × riversleaianum A low-growing geranium for the front of the border or the rock garden, this hybrid has grey-green foliage and flowers ranging from pink to deep magenta on different plants. It has a trailing habit and will scramble about among other plants, covering the ground between them.

Geranium × magnificum in summer

Among the best varieties are *G. × r.* 'Mavis Simpson', with flowers of a silvery shell-pink, and *G. × r.* 'Russell Prichard', with deep magenta flowers. Height 30cm/12in, spread 90cm/36in. Zone 7

Geranium sanguineum The bloody cranesbill has flowers of an intense magenta that contrast well with the smooth, finely divided dark green leaves. The foliage goes red in autumn. *G.s.* var. *striatum* (syn. *G.s.* var. *lancastrense*) is a form with pale pink flowers. Height 25cm/10in, spread 45cm/18in. Another good plant of similar size and habit is *G. cinereum* var. *subcaulescens,* which has magenta flowers with black centres, and soft silvery-green leaves. Zone 4

Geranium wallichianum 'Buxton's Variety' Flowering over a long period in late summer, this geranium has a trailing habit and will scramble through shrubs and over low walls. The flowers are a gorgeous pale blue with white centres. Zone 6

Another extended performance, this one lasting the whole year. The blue oat grass, *Helictotrichon sempervirens,* makes a good cornerstone to a herbaceous border in which all the other perennials wax and wane at different intervals, many of them dying off above ground in winter. The grass loses some of its leaves, but enough survive over winter for it to be regarded as an evergreen. It is a good idea to comb through the tufts in spring to clear out the dead leaves.

Helictotrichon sempervirens

BLUE OAT GRASS

Evergreen tufts of blue-green foliage,
graceful summer flower heads

The ornamental grasses and the grass-like sedges tend to be the great workhorses of the border, whose virtues are unsung. They may not display the obvious glamour of some neighbouring plants, but they have a grace and charm that are a source of lasting pleasure in the garden. All are grown principally for their handsome foliage, and between them they offer an astonishing diversity of leaf colour, texture, size and form. According to your taste and the size of your plot you have a choice ranging in colour from yellow to silvery blue, plain or variegated, and in all sizes from towering giants to tiny dwarf forms. Some of them have splendid architectural presence and these are ideal for use as punctuation marks at key points in the garden.

One of the most useful 'punctuation' grasses is the blue oat grass, *Helictotrichon sempervirens*, which makes a dense rounded clump of narrow, arching, pale grey-green leaves that are rather hard and spiky to the touch. As it is evergreen, the clump is a striking feature throughout the seasons. In summer the dainty flower heads are borne well above the foliage, making an attractive secondary feature. Later, they dry well for flower arrangements.

The naturally rounded form of this plant makes it an obvious candidate for a corner position in a border, where it will serve the architectural function of a pivot or cornerstone. If you have a blue or silver border so much the better, because the metallic quality of the grass makes it an ideal companion to plants in this colour range. Like many grasses, it also looks good growing in gravel or among pebbles.

• The foliage makes a mound about 90cm/36in high and 1.2m/4ft across, and the flowers reach about 1.5m/5ft. *H. sempervirens* does not have runners and so it is not in the least invasive. It needs full sun and well-drained soil though it is not particular whether the soil is acid or alkaline. The clump does not die back in winter, but individual leaves do die and so they need to be combed out to keep the plant tidy. Propagate by division of the clump in spring; as with all grasses, if division is attempted in autumn the clump may rot with winter damp. Zone 4

OTHER GRASSES TO GROW

Carex elata 'Aurea' Of all grass-like plants, Bowles' golden sedge is probably the brightest yellow. An attractive plant, it is named after the English horticulturist E.A. Bowles, who discovered it as a mutant of an undistinguished wild sedge grass. The narrow, arching leaves are golden yellow with the narrowest margin of green. This is variable and there is a form that some gardeners would find preferable, with golden leaves lacking the green margin. The flowers are black tufts, covered with golden-brown anthers. The foliage makes a clump up to 60cm/24in in height and spread, with the flowers a little taller.

Carex elata 'Aurea' colours up best in full sun; in shade it is bright green. However it likes plenty of moisture, and does well in a poolside planting. Here it would provide a delightful contrast of textures with the same-coloured bog-loving *Iris pseudacorus* 'Variegata'. Propagate by division in spring. Zone 5

Cortaderia selloana Queen of all the grasses, pampas grass is so often grown in the wrong place that it has got a bad name. Its hulking tussocks, 1.8m/6ft in height and spread, consisting of sharply serrated leaves, are simply not suitable for the small suburban garden. On a grand scale, however, there is nothing to beat them as eye-catchers. I have seen pampas grasses grown *en masse* beside the huge lake at Sheffield Park in Sussex, their great plumes like sails

Carex elata 'Aurea'

reflecting in the water against a shimmering backcloth of orange and gold autumn colours. They would look spectacular planted in an avenue at the entrance to an estate. In an attempt to squeeze this stately plant into the small gardens market, plant breeders have introduced miniature versions, but to my eye these will always look like freaks. There are, however, forms with variegated leaves, adding an extra attraction to an already attractive plant, and these grow shorter than the type, with their flower plumes reaching 1.8m/6ft as opposed to an average 3m/10ft in the larger varieties. *C.s.* 'Aureolineata' (sometimes sold as 'Gold Band') has leaves with yellow margins. The form 'Albolineata' (often known as 'Silver Stripe') has the equivalent variegation in white. Among several available full-size forms of pampas grass, the most desirable is probably *C.s.* 'Sunningdale Silver', which has sturdy flowers like silver banners 3m/10ft above the ground. All these cortaderias flower in autumn. If you are looking for a pampas grass to flower in summer, try *C. richardii*, which has plumes up to 2.5m/8ft.

In all cortaderias, male and female flowers grow on separate plants. The females are preferable, having the more bushy flower plumes. All cortaderias demand an open site in full sun, and well-drained soil. They will not do well in clay. Although the plant could be described as evergreen, a substantial number of leaves do die each season, and the

Planting on a grand scale. This 'hedge' of *Cortaderia selloana* 'Sunningdale Silver' stretches for over 100m/350ft. The plumes, 3m/10ft high, are bending under a heavy burden of hoar frost. This enormous pampas grass looks quite wonderful in winter, though strong winds and heavy snows will take their toll of the feathery plumes. A double row of pampas grass, on either side of an entrance drive, is a feasible alternative to an avenue of trees.

centre of the plant can become clogged with dead material. The best way to deal with this is to cut back all the foliage in early spring; be sure to wear strong gloves. Some gardeners counsel setting fire to the old foliage, but this is risky as it is impossible to avoid damaging the new growth. To propagate, divide the clump with a spade in early spring. Zone 8

Festuca glauca The blue fescue has silvery-blue foliage making a tuft of 30cm/12in height and spread. The flower heads are the same silvery colour when they appear in midsummer, though they fade and dry to a pale creamy brown. A classic ingredient of the silver border, it looks marvellous when grown with plants of a similar colour but contrasting texture, such as lamb's ears, *Stachys byzantina* (syn. *S. lanata*), which has soft velvety leaves of silver-grey.

This grass needs full sun and well-drained soil to attain its silvery-blue colour; it is much more green when grown in shade, and in soggy ground the plant will rot and die. Propagate by division in spring. Zone 5

Milium effusum **'Aureum'** The fresh lime-green of Bowles' golden grass brings a glow of light to a shady corner of the garden. It has flat tapering leaves that are quite slack and bend gracefully under their own weight. They make a loose mound, about 45cm/18in height and spread, with a wispy halo of delicate yellow flower heads reaching perhaps 30cm/12in above the foliage in summer. Use this grass as an underplanting for green-flowered shrubs or perennials, such as euphorbias. It also makes a wonderful foil for purple flowers such as those of *Viola* 'Huntercombe Purple'.

In the wild *M. effusum* is a woodland plant and the golden version also prefers dappled shade, although it will thrive on any soil. It will spread by seeding itself, if you allow it, and you can also propagate it by division in spring. Zone 5

Miscanthus sinensis A grass for a sunny position at the back of the border, *M. sinensis* makes a tall and graceful clump of 2.5m/8ft or more in height, 1.2m/4ft in spread. The leaves are up to 90cm/36in long, fanning out from bamboo-like stalks. They whisper among themselves in the slightest breeze. If you are waiting for a hedge to grow behind a border, a few clumps of this grass will be a temporary expedient to tide you over. It reaches its full height in a season, and dies back in winter. The dead winter foliage, veiled with hoar frost, is perhaps even more beautiful than the plant in full fling in summer. It would be a crime to cut it back until the cycle of new growth begins again in spring.

There are some interesting variegated forms. 'Cabaret' is perhaps the most striking white-edged cultivar. 'Zebrinus' and 'Strictus' both have irregular patterns of horizontal cream stripes across the leaves. Propagate by division in spring. The species is hardy to zone 6, variegated cultivars to zone 7.

Pennisetum orientale A delightful small grass for the front of a border, *P. orientale* produces a mass of pink tufted flower heads, rather like the tails of small squirrels. The flower heads appear in the late summer and last well into autumn, and so this grass is a good accompaniment for Michaelmas daisies or dahlias. Its feathery texture would also make a fitting contrast with the flat slabs of sedum flowers. And it looks striking grown in quantity as a specimen plant. Pennisetum reaches up to 75cm/30in height and spread. The leaves are dark green, flat and arching.

Clumps of *Pennisetum orientale* make a fringe at the front of an autumn border of dahlias, Michaelmas daisies and salvias. Grasses, with their neutral-coloured flowers, make good partners for almost any border plants. Most grasses put on their peak performance in summer, but pennisetums flower in autumn.

A sturdy clump of *Phalaris arundinacea* var. *picta* (gardener's garters) with a fringe of *Alchemilla mollis*.

This grass is a perennial for any soil, but it must have full sun. It is not reliably hardy, so it is a good idea to take some offsets in autumn and keep them under the protection of a cold frame over winter.

Another attractive pennisetum is *P. villosum*, known as feathertop. Its diaphanous flower heads are like loose stubby feathers that bounce back the light. Height and spread 60cm/24in. *P. orientale* is hardy to zone 6, *P. villosum* to zone 8.

Phalaris arundinacea var. picta Gardener's garters is one of the most commonly grown grasses, but none the worse for that. The loosely arching leaves are strongly patterned with dark green and white stripes that run along their length. The plant forms a clump 75cm/30in high with flowers 60cm/24in higher. It will thrive in any soil, in full sun or part-shade, and it is a useful plant to provide a touch of light to a dim corner of the border, but be warned – it can be very invasive. 'Feesey' is a good creamy-white variegated variety, paler than *P.a.* var. *picta* and less invasive. Propagate by division in spring. Zone 4

Helleborus argutifolius

Bold evergreen foliage, green flowers in early spring

You can become addicted to hellebores. Grow a few and you will crave more. The more familiar you become with them, the more you will appreciate the distinctions between the different species and forms. As your taste for them becomes increasingly refined you will enjoy the most modest and subtle varieties – those with small flowers in shades of green – which you would probably never even have noticed in the early stages of your gardening career. At some time quite early in the process of hellebore addiction you may become aware of one of the tallest and most striking plants of the group, *Helleborus argutifolius*, also called *H. corsicus* after the Mediterranean island which is its place of origin.

Helleborus argutifolius is the best of the genus for foliage. The evergreen leaves are held high on thick, arching stalks. They are grey-green in colour and smooth to the touch. Each leaf is divided into three leaflets which have serrated edges like a fine saw. The plant has a two-year cycle, with each stem producing only foliage in its first year, and flowers developing on the mature stems in the spring of the second year. After flowering the stems die back to make room for new growth. Replacement stems will arise from the base, and so the plant counts as a herbaceous perennial rather than a biennial. The same plant will survive for many years.

The flowers are inconspicuous in colour but perfect in form. They are cups of the palest green, with yellow anthers that radiate from the centre and arch across the bowl of each cup. The flowers are long-lasting on the plant, but it is difficult to preserve hellebores as cut flowers. Some flower arrangers advocate plunging the base of the stems in boiling water. Others make 8–10cm/3–4in slits in the stems and soak the flowers up to their necks in water overnight before arranging them.

• Height to 90cm/36in, spread to 1.2m/4ft. The top-heavy foliage may need discreet staking. Hellebores like shade or part-shade and rich, well-drained, moist soil. They seed themselves readily, and if you have several different species and forms of hellebore in the garden they are bound to inter-breed, to give you a whole range of unpredictable hybrids. Zone 7

OTHER HELLEBORES TO GROW

Helleborus foetidus Another green hellebore, with arching racemes of hooded pale lime-coloured flowers, usually edged with a thin rim of crimson. They appear first in late winter and last well into the spring. Finely cut leaves of the darkest green. Height 60cm/24in, spread 45cm/18in. Useful ground cover, particularly beneath shrubs of winter interest, such as coppiced willows or the rubus species with striking stems. Zone 5

Helleborus niger The Christmas rose is not a rose and only rarely flowers in time for Christmas, but it is otherwise perfectly named. Its Latin name of *niger* refers to its black roots, but it would have been more appropriate for it to have been given a name that celebrates its pure white flowers. These are large, about 6cm/2½in across, but the plant is relatively small, rarely reaching more than 30cm/12in in height and spread. The form 'Potter's Wheel' has larger flowers and more of them. Zone 3

A sturdy plant of *Helleborus argutifolius* fills a border in spring. The flowers open from midwinter onwards and last for about three months. The stiff evergreen foliage gives good value for the rest of the year. This garden is cleverly laid out for all-year interest. The infrastructure of box hedges, punctuated with terracotta amphorae, is decorated with unusual standard forsythias, pruned into bobbles.

Helleborus niger in early spring

Helleborus orientalis Among the loveliest of early spring flowers, the Lenten rose has received a great deal of attention from plant hunters and breeders. They have produced strains with flowers which range in colour from pure white, through cream to primrose-yellow, pink and plum-crimson verging on black. Whatever colour takes your fancy you can be sure to enjoy exquisitely beautiful cup-shaped flowers. Some recent cultivars have upward-facing flowers, but I still prefer those that are demurely downward-nodding, though you have to turn them up to appreciate the delicate markings on their faces – some forms are plain but many are freckled with patterns of crimson dots. To highlight the flowers in spring it is best to cut away the tired old foliage. Fresh young foliage will grow up from the base. Height and spread 45cm/18in. Propagate by division or by seed – but if you want seed to come true to type you will need to choose the parents carefully. Left to their own devices these hellebores are totally promiscuous and will interbreed with abandon. Zone 4

Helleborus orientalis in spring

Hosta sieboldiana elegans

PLANTAIN LILY

Architectural foliage from spring to autumn, summer flower spikes

Grown primarily for their succulent and graceful foliage, hostas also produce elegant spikes of flowers reminiscent of lilies. Some of them give, in addition, good (though brief) autumn colour. Another virtue of hostas is the discreet way in which they die back in winter. The first frost of autumn transforms the leaves into a pathetic mound like melted plastic, with hardly any unsightly dead stubs to wither and rot. Above ground the plant vanishes almost completely. Only the roots remain, poised to deliver a new crop of succulent young crowns in spring.

There are several hundred named species and varieties of hosta, and with such a wide choice of excellent plants it is difficult to limit a recommendation to only a few. In choosing hostas you will need to think about your preferences for leaf colour and shape, plain or variegated leaves, tall or short plants. If you have sufficient room, why not consider one of the largest and most dramatic among them, *Hosta sieboldiana* var. *elegans*?

This hosta produces a magnificent mound of blue-green foliage up to 1m/39in high if it has room, with a spread of 1.5m/5ft in an unrestricted space. The leaves are enormous – about 45cm/18in long and 30cm/12in wide, splaying out from a fleshy leaf stalk about 60cm/24in long. Heart-shaped in silhouette, they are scalloped and folded into sculptural forms. Numerous veins radiate from the midriff to follow the curved shape of the leaf, and between them are prominent ridges that give a crinkled texture. After rain, droplets of water collect in the veins or run off the leaves like balls of mercury. The delicate blue-grey tone of the leaf comes from a white bloom that covers its upper and lower surfaces. This bloom comes off easily to reveal

Hosta sieboldiana 'Frances Williams' in summer

RIGHT Yellow echoes between *Hosta fortunei aureomarginata* and the yellow-leaved *Choisya ternata* 'Sundance' further back in the border. The pink flower between them is *Geranium endressii*.

OPPOSITE In a shaded border, *Hosta sieboldiana* var. *elegans* dominates a group of ferns, a large clump of *Geranium* × *magnificum,* and a blue-leaved *Sedum rhodiola rosea,* cleverly planted as a companion.

the dark green surface below, so the leaves are quickly spoilt by fingering.

In midsummer the flower spikes protrude just above the foliage. The narrow, funnel-shaped flowers are lilac-grey in colour, and open from the bottom of the spike upwards. Although they are a fitting complement to the foliage, they do have one inherent disadvantage. By the time the flowers at the top of the spike have opened, those lower down have faded and died. Unfortunately, they do not die gracefully. The first shower of rain will knock off the dead flowers, which then proceed to stick to the leaves below. This can ruin the appearance of the foliage and you may make it worse if you attempt to pluck off the decaying flowers, thus marking the leaf surfaces. The best way out, sadly, is to remove the

flower heads altogether as soon as the first flowers begin to go over.

One of the best grey-leaved foliage plants, *H.s.* var. *elegans* is a star turn in the silver border, provided it can be accorded part-shade and plenty of moisture. In this respect it differs from the majority of silver plants, which prefer full sun, and it is a test for the gardener's ingenuity to provide suitable conditions for different neighbouring plants. Grey foliage is useful in other contexts too, and this hosta provides an excellent neutral foil for plants whose colours might otherwise appear too strident, such as the magnificent magenta *Geranium psilostemon*. Again, it takes its place as one of the mainstays of a corner of the garden devoted to foliage. The hosta's great wavy dinner-plate leaves make a marvellous contrast with the filigree foliage of larger ferns, such as *Matteuccia struthiopteris* – and they both favour the same conditions of moist part-shade. Hostas are also ideal plants for underplanting with spring flowers – celandines, wood anemones, snowdrops all grow marvellously with them and start to die back as the leaves of the hostas unfurl.

• This hosta will thrive in a shaded or part-shaded position in any fertile soil, but it must be kept moist; the edge of a pond or boggy area is ideal. It will survive in full sun, but the grey bloom on the leaves will be less effective and they will appear a darker green. It needs to be fed regularly. It shares its favoured damp conditions with its worst pests, snails and slugs, which find the juicy leaves and stems irresistible. Uncontrolled, they will devastate the leaves with unsightly holes and if you love hostas you will have to wage war on these molluscs without sentimentality. Propagate hostas by division: the best way is simply to cut a slice out of the mature clump with a spade as if you were cutting a cake. This should be done in spring as the crowns are just appearing above the soil. Zone 3

Companionable foliage. *Hosta crispula* makes a centrepiece in a green and white composition that includes *Dicentra spectabilis alba, Brunnera macrophylla* 'Dawson's White' (with blue flowers) and a single white star of *Ornithogalum umbellatum.*

OTHER HOSTAS TO GROW

Hosta sieboldiana 'Frances Williams' Also known under the name of 'Gold Edge', this hosta is a sport of *H.s.* var. *elegans*, first noticed by Mrs Frances Williams in a nursery bed in Connecticut in 1936. She recognized the value of this oddity with glaucous leaves and broad yellow margins. This pattern is most marked in young growth, and by the end of the season the two tones are hardly distinguishable. Unfortunately, the leaves tend to decay earlier in the autumn than those of other hostas. They may be somewhat unstable as a result of the plant's origin as a sport. This hosta reaches a height and spread of 1m/39in. Zone 3

Hosta crispula An elegant hosta with narrow leaf stalks and wavy, white-edged leaves that taper to a fine point. The leaves have pronounced leaf veins that add to the complexity of the surface pattern. Height to 75cm/30in, spread 90cm/36in. Zone 3

Hosta fortunei This graceful hosta has finely pointed, fresh green, wavy-edged leaves. It makes a mound of up to 75cm/30in high with a spread of 90cm/36in. The lilac-coloured flowers are held on tall spikes well above the foliage. There are several attractive variegated forms available including *H.f.* var. *albopicta*, in which the central segments of the leaves are variably patterned with light green and cream. *H.f.* 'Albomarginata', as its name suggests, has white margins to its leaves, and, similarly, *H.f. aureomarginata* has yellow margins. Zone 3

Hosta plantaginea An exception among hostas in its preference for full sun, this is one of the few hostas to flourish in a Mediterranean climate. It has broad, shiny, lime-green leaves, but its flowers take on more importance than those of other hostas by virtue of their sweet scent. The flowers, produced in late summer, are pure white and open fully at night, when they release maximum scent. This hosta is a good candidate for growing in a pot, which can be moved to nosing distance when the flowers appear. Height 60cm/24in, spread 75cm/30in. Zone 3

Hosta ventricosa An excellent hosta with heart-shaped mid-green leaves, making a graceful mound 75cm/30in high with a spread of 1.2m/4ft. The flower tubes are a bulging bell shape, and they are a deep lilac colour. There are two excellent variegated forms of the same dimensions, *H.v.* var. *aureomaculata,* in which the young leaves are strikingly marked with yellow, and *H.v.* 'Aureomarginata' (syn. *H.v.* 'Variegata'), which has leaves edged with cream. Zone 3

Iris foetidissima

GLADWYN OR STINKING IRIS

Evergreen leaves, summer flowers, orange autumn
berries lasting through the winter

As a general rule irises are ephemeral flowers. The
most glamorous types, the bearded irises, take up a
lot of space in the garden for the sake of ten brief
days of glory in early summer. So any iris that extends its season with a double act is especially welcome. *Iris foetidissima* does just that.

It has to be said that the first part of the performance is rather modest. The flowers are characteristi-
cally iris-shaped, but compared with their bearded
cousins they are dingy in colour. Though there is
considerable variety among them, all have tones of
creamy yellow and dull purple mixed in different
proportions. The most attractive are to be found in a
variety called *citrina*, in which the yellow element
predominates,

The chief glory of *I. foetidissima* is in the seedheads.
The parts of an iris flower come in threes, and the
seedheads are no exception. They are formed of
three separate lobes which swell throughout the
summer until in autumn they split along their

seams. The flamboyant orange berries do not spill
out but remain attached, come wind, rain and snow,
for much of the winter.

This iris has yet another interesting feature, in its
dense clump of evergreen leaves. It is the foliage that
earns the plant its name of *foetidissima*, or 'stinking
iris', because when crushed it gives off an acrid smell
(said, by those who have imagination in these mat-
ters, to be reminiscent of roast beef).

● Height and spread 75cm/30in. This plant is a
great survivor, tolerant of sun or shade and damp or
dry conditions. Propagate by division or by seed.
Zone 7

Iris foetidissima in winter

Iris foetidissima in summer

Lamium maculatum roseum

PINK DEAD-NETTLE

Silver-patterned leaves, pink flowers in
late spring and summer

The dead-nettles, so called because they lack the
sting of their pestilential lookalikes, are quintessen-
tial ground-cover plants. Put them under trees and
shrubs where hardly anything else will grow and they
will perform for you with little further trouble. They
will also thrive in part-shade at the feet of herbaceous perennials and bulbs. You only need to inter-
vene when they get above their station and begin to
encroach upon your prime border plantings.

There are countless varieties of dead-nettles,
named for their flower colour or leaf pattern, and
Lamium maculatum roseum is one among several
favourites. The flowers are pale pink and appear first
in late spring and again intermittently throughout
the summer. The first flush coincides with the last of
the tulips and an effective treatment is to grow the
pink peony-flowered tulip 'Angélique' through a
carpet of pink lamium. If you are lucky there will still
be flowers on the plants to accompany pink and
magenta geraniums and roses at midsummer.

The lamium's leaves are crossed by a multiplicity
of ribs, giving them a wrinkled texture. They are
dark green and marked with a variable broad silvery-
grey stripe down the centre. This attractive variegation gives the plant the sparkle that makes it ideal to
brighten up a shady corner under a tree.

Other attractive forms of *L. maculatum* include
L.m. album, which has pure white flowers. 'Beacon
Silver' has leaves in which the variegation has taken
over the whole surface so that they are pure silver,
with just a suggestion of pink at the edges; the

No bare soil to be seen.
Lamium maculatum roseum
makes a thick carpet
around the feet of *Knautia
macedonica* and annual
larkspurs.

flowers are dark pink. *L.m.* 'White Nancy' has similar leaves but white flowers. The variety *L.m.* 'Aureum' has yellow-variegated leaves; it needs to be in shade or part-shade because, as with yellow-leaved cultivars of many plants, the sun tends to brown the leaves.

● Height 23cm/9in, spread 40cm/15in. Any soil. Shade or part-shade. The plant propagates itself by putting out roots at points where the stems touch the ground, and it will also set seed. Zone 3

ANOTHER LAMIUM TO GROW

Lamium galeobdolon 'Florentinum' A more vigorous and invasive ground cover than *L. maculatum*, *L. galeobdolon* 'Florentinum' (syn. 'Variegatum') is nevertheless to be recommended for a wild area on account of its exceptionally beautiful foliage. Each leaf is like a heart-shaped artist's palette, marked with a central dab of green, with freehand swashes of pure silver on either side. The flower spikes are yellow. Zone 4

Lamium maculatum 'White Nancy'

Making effective ground cover beneath a Rugosa rose, *Lamium maculatum album* intermingles with *Geranium sanguineum*. This should be the limit of its spread – if the lamium encroaches further and threatens to strangle the geranium it will need to be suppressed.

Planted beside a house wall, *Lavatera* 'Barnsley' receives some protection from winds that could snap its brittle stems. Next to the lavatera a container holds a selection of tender perennials and annuals, planted for a single season. Chosen to harmonize with the pale pink of the lavatera, they include the tender *Verbena* 'Silver Anne' and two pink forms of annual cosmos, as well as an ornamental cabbage tucked in beneath them.

Lavatera 'Barnsley'

TREE MALLOW

Shell-pink flowers all summer, persisting
until the first autumn frosts

There is a story behind most of the named cultivars with which we populate our gardens. Some of the names have become blurred by history, but with *Lavatera* 'Barnsley' we have a new plant of our own time, named after the village of Barnsley in Gloucestershire, where the distinguished garden designer and writer Rosemary Verey has created her unique garden at Barnsley House. The story goes that Mrs Verey spotted the plant growing in the garden of a friend. She took a few cuttings and grew plants on at Barnsley House.

The feature that distinguishes 'Barnsley' from other lavateras is the delicate shell-pink colour of its flowers. Their shape is typical of mallow flowers, cup-shaped with wavy-edged petals – somewhere between a hibiscus and a hollyhock. At the throat of the flower, where each petal tapers to a narrow base, the colour darkens to deep rose, giving the flowers an attractive bicoloured effect. The flowers line the many-branching stems and in a good season the plant is covered with a mass of blooms for some five months from midsummer to early autumn. Individually the flowers do not last long, but no sooner has one withered and dropped than another bud has opened to take its place. They die gracefully, and drop to the ground, where they can be swept up if necessary.

A versatile filler for the end of the season. Easily grown from seed sown in spring, annual *Lavatera trimestris* 'Mont Blanc' is useful for filling spaces left by earlier-flowering bulbs or perennials. Here a mass of it has been planted to fill an area of the garden that had been left fallow.

Alcea rosea in summer

The plant does present problems, however, in the brittleness of its stems. It tends to grow bigger and faster than is good for it. It can put on over 1.8m/6ft of growth in a single season, with stems the size of a man's wrist at their base. The weight of the branches may split the stems, and strong winds will make this problem worse. I favour planting it against a wall or fence for support. You can tie hoops of strong twine at different heights around the plant to hold the branches in (but don't tie them so tightly as to restrict its natural growth). In cold areas the wall will give some winter protection too. This lavatera is vulnerable to heavy frosts, which may cut it back to the ground. This is not necessarily the disaster that it sounds, because pruning right back in spring is recommended practice (see below).

• Height and spread to 2.5m/8ft. Full sun in any well-drained soil. Feed well for best results. To prevent the main stems splitting, support the plant with a stake, or tie against a wall; thin the branches if they become too top-heavy. The plant has a tendency to revert to its dark pink ancestral form: cut out any reverting branches. In winter, I recommend tying up the plant with protective hessian, against winds and frosts. The upper growth will itself give some frost protection to the base of the plant. In spring, cut right back to within 45cm/18in of the ground. This plant does not have a long life expectancy – four or five years at the most – so take cuttings in late summer to ensure that you have replacements if needed the following spring. Propagation can only be achieved by cuttings; seeds will not grow true to type. Zone 8

OTHER MALLOWS TO GROW

The family Malvaceae includes several distinct genera, some of them perennials, some biennials or annuals, some (like *Lavatera* 'Barnsley') capable, in a favoured climate, of growing as shrubs, but all plants having the distinctive mallow flower shape. The following are among the best.

Lavatera maritima An attractive tree mallow that has pale pink flowers with magenta centres. Its grey-green leaves have serrated edges, but are quite soft to the touch. It is smaller than *Lavatera* 'Barnsley', reaching a height and spread of 1.5m/5ft, and it begins flowering rather later in the summer. Unfortunately, being a plant from the Mediterranean, it is not reliably hardy in colder regions, and needs to be overwintered as cuttings under glass. Zone 9

Lavatera trimestris **'Mont Blanc'** A bushy annual, of height 75cm/30in, spread 50cm/20in, with

Lavatera maritima in summer

trumpet-shaped flowers of purest white. Easily grown from seed sown in spring in the site where it is to flower, or grown under glass and transplanted. Thrives in pure sun. Collect the nobbly seedheads when ripe and the seeds should come true. *L. trimestris* is available in other colours, notably 'Silver Cup', but do not be deceived by this name; it is not silver at all, but a rather aggressive shade of knicker-pink. Zone 8

Alcea rosea One of the delights of the typical cottage garden, hollyhocks produce tall spires up to 2.5m/8ft high of flowers in a range of colours from white, through pale yellow to pink to mauve to deep purplish black. Hollyhocks are biennials, easily grown from seed. Zone 3

Malva moschata The musk mallow, so called because of the scent given off by the leaves when crushed, is a short-lived perennial. This means that plants are best replaced every other year by new stock grown from seed. Growing to a height of 90cm/36in and spread of 50cm/20in it is a delicately pretty plant, with fine-cut, fern-like leaves and frilly-edged pink flowers. There is a white form, *M.m. alba*, also highly desirable. Like other mallows, *M. moschata* needs full sun, but it will not tolerate poor soil. Zone 3

Sidalcea malviflora One of the most elegant of the mallows, with spikes up to a height of 1.2m/4ft and spread of 45cm/18in of clean-cut, saucer-shaped, clear pink flowers, like miniature hollyhocks. The cultivar 'Loveliness' lives up to its name, with flowers of a delicate shell-pink. The plant has two kinds of foliage; the leaves at the base grow in clumps and are broad and rounded, whereas those attached to the stems are narrow and lobed. A perennial, requiring full sun, it can be propagated by division or from seed. Zone 3

Sidalcea malviflora in summer

Lunaria annua

HONESTY

Spring flowers, followed by silvery seedheads
that last all winter

Honesty must have earned its charming name from its habit of extending its coin-shaped seedpods openly throughout the winter. The seedcases glow silver in the low winter light, looking especially good with a sprinkling of snowdrops beneath them, a colourless frosty picture that sums up the season.

Lunaria pays its dues in spring too, and for my money I prefer the form with white flowers and variegated leaves, *Lunaria annua* 'Alba Variegata'. The flowers add a touch of brilliance to the spring border, bringing light to a shady corner and combining happily with tulips of any colour. The mature leaves have a sprinkling of white around their heart-shaped edges, as if their rims have been dipped in thick cream. This leaf pattern complements the white flowers to give a plant that positively sparkles.

Flower arrangers value lunaria for dried flower displays, and they commonly titivate cut stems by picking off the outer seedcases. The seeds are sandwiched between three paper-thin layers of transparent tissue. The two outer layers can easily be stripped off, releasing the seeds and leaving the central partition still attached to the stem to make a far brighter display than the full three-layered seedpods. I would counsel gardeners to do the same to plants *in situ*. It is a time-consuming business, but it is the only way to collect seed, and you are improving the winter display into the bargain. I find that it is a task that I can give to my children without the fear of putting them off gardening for life. They have a satisfying harvest of seeds and they can see at the end that they have enhanced the appearance of the plant.

• Height up to 75cm/30in, spread 40cm/15in. Sun or part-shade, any soil. Obtain seed from a reliable

Lunaria annua 'Alba Variegata' in spring

source, to ensure that you get the right colour. Once you have lunaria in the garden it will readily seed itself but, as it is a biennial, you will need to make a second sowing of seed one year after the first, to guarantee an annual succession of plants. The white-flowered and variegated forms come true from seed, but only when the plants are completely isolated from other types. Do not be discouraged if the young plants show no variegation in their first year; the patterning will be distinct by the time they come to flower. Zone 4

ANOTHER LUNARIA TO GROW

Lunaria rediviva The perennial lunaria has white flowers similar to those of *L. annua*, with the added virtue of a delicate scent. Height and spread to 75cm/30in. Zone 6

In late autumn, the seedheads of honesty *(Lunaria annua)* accompany the berries of the Oregon grape *(Mahonia aquifolium).* The honesty will seed itself and the mahonia will spread by suckers. The two plants need very little attention, and will keep their little plot of ground decoratively covered for many a year.

Matteuccia struthiopteris in winter

Matteuccia struthiopteris

SHUTTLECOCK FERN, OSTRICH FERN

Attractive foliage from spring to autumn, with decorative plumes lasting through the winter

There are few more potent symbols of spring than the sight of fern fronds uncurling. They seem to contain the potential energy of watchsprings. Add a sprinkling of daffodils to the fresh sap-green of the ferns and you have the very image of spring.

From the vast range of ferns available, *Matteuccia struthiopteris*, the shuttlecock fern, is a good choice to begin with, because it has something to offer in every season, including winter. In spring each clump is renewed by a circle of young fronds, facing inwards. As they unfurl they bend outwards, so that the plant assumes a hollow shuttlecock shape.

In summer matteuccia produces reproductive fronds which are quite distinct from its other foliage. These fronds, which produce spores, rise, upright and bushy, from the centre of the fern. Although they go brown they remain through the winter, after the rest of the foliage has died back.

● Like most ferns, matteuccia needs moist conditions. It grows well beside ponds and streams and is an ideal candidate for the bog garden. It prefers sunny situations, but will survive full shade. Zone 5

Matteuccia struthiopteris unfurling in spring

Osmunda regalis fronds

Asplenium scolopendrium

Dryopteris filix-mas in spring

OTHER FERNS TO GROW

Asplenium scolopendrium (syn. *Phyllitis scolopendrium*) The evergreen hart's-tongue fern, with its characteristic strap-shaped fronds, makes a plant of height 75cm/30in. Prefers neutral or acid soil and will grow in crevices or rock gardens. Zone 4

Asplenium trichomanes The maidenhair spleenwort is a small creeping fern, with a spread of only 30cm/12in, which readily colonizes walls and rocky crevices. It has delicately divided fronds. Sun or part-shade, tolerant of seaside conditions. Zone 4

Dryopteris filix-mas The male fern is a robust deciduous woodland fern, common in the wild over a wide range of Europe and northern parts of the United States, but none the worse for that. Tufts of elegantly divided fronds reach a height and spread of 1.2m/4ft. Requires moist soil rich in humus, in shade or part-shade. Zone 4

Osmunda regalis One of the tallest and most stately ferns, the royal fern has broad fronds with finger-sized divisions. It produces plumes of brown-coloured fertile fronds. The foliage turns golden brown in autumn. Prefers neutral or acid soil, and likes damp conditions. Ideal for a waterside planting, where it may reach a height of 1.8m/6ft and a spread of 3m/10ft. Zone 3

Polystichum setiferum The semi-evergreen soft shield fern is among the most elegant of the hardy ferns, with intricately divided arching fronds which tend to make a ground-hugging shield-shaped tuft of height 50cm/20in and spread 90cm/36in. There are countless varieties, among the best of which is 'Divisilobum', which has fronds that are especially finely divided. Shade or part-shade, any soil with plenty of humus. Zone 5

Meconopsis cambrica

Meconopsis cambrica

WELSH POPPY

Yellow flowers appearing over summer and autumn

Not to be confused with its stately blue cousins from the Himalayas, which can be very difficult to grow, the Welsh poppy is disarmingly easy. Simply beg a seedhead or two from a gardener who has the plant, scatter some seed in odd corners of the garden and off you go. Once established, it will seed itself at the edge of paths and in undisturbed corners of beds to give an informal 'lived-in' look to the garden. The flower comes in two colours, lemon-yellow and orange, and both come true from seed. I strongly urge you to choose the yellow and dispense with the orange, which is rather a strident colour and diffi-cult to associate with other plants. The yellow variety fits in well with herbs and vegetables, and makes a cheerful contrast with low blue plants, such as the veronicas and blue omphalodes. However, being a self-seeder it is not a flower for careful plantsmanship, but rather for informal general effect. It is particularly effective for lighting up dark corners under trees or in shaded areas of the garden; not grown *en masse* but as a dot plant, springing up here and there.

● Height 30cm/12in, spread 20cm/8in. Any soil, sun or shade. Seeds scattered in spring should flower the same summer and reseed for a further show. Autumn sowings will produce late spring flowers. Zone 6

Morina longifolia

Handsome foliage, white and pink summer flowers persisting as seedheads

Morina is one of those perfect perennials – attractive in all its parts and at all stages of its growth. The foliage is thistle-like, making a rosette of narrow, prickly leaves near ground level. Rising from the centre of the rosette in midsummer are spires of delicate white flowers arranged in whorls around the stems. The flowers are tubular and change in colour in the course of their development from almost pure white to varying shades of pink.

Being predominantly white, the flowers look well with almost any companion colours, including blues, lilacs and yellows. You might choose to high-light the pink touch to the flowers by partnering them with a pink geranium such as *Geranium endressii* 'Wargrave Pink', whose softly rounded habit will contrast satisfyingly with the morina's spiny erect form.

The flowers die off without any fuss, simply dropping discreetly to the ground and leaving the striking, spiny seedheads to mature. Their tall silhouettes make a valuable contribution to the autumn bounty in the border. Then they can be gathered, dried off and kept as everlasting flowers.

● Height 75cm/30in, spread 18in/45cm. Needs a mild climate, full sun and well-drained soil; will do well in sandy conditions. Propagate by division after flowering or by seed. Zone 8

Morina longifolia seedheads

Adding height at the front of a colourful border, a clump of *Morina longifolia* dominates potentillas, mimulus and *Geranium endressii*. After the other, brighter flowers have passed over the morina will still be giving value with its attractive seedheads.

Paeonia mlokosewitschii
in early spring

Paeonia mlokosewitschii
in mid-spring

Paeonia mlokosewitschii
in autumn

Paeonia mlokosewitschii in late spring

Paeonia mlokosewitschii
Attractive foliage, primrose-yellow flowers
in late spring, autumn fruits

As far as flowers go, the herbaceous peonies are among the prima donnas of the border, most of them giving a sensational but short-lived display, which often coincides with that of those other shooting stars, the old-fashioned roses. However, all have attractive cut-leaved foliage which makes up for the ephemeral appearance of the flowers. Aristocrat among this large group is the peony with the unpronounceable name *Paeonia mlokosewitschii*, often memorized by despairing gardeners as 'Molly the Witch'. For sheer quality of flower, foliage and autumn fruits, she stands head and shoulders above

the rest, with something to offer for every season. In early spring the first shoots appear – dark crimson spears of unfolding leaves. These look good with hybrid red primroses and polyanthus – an appropriate association because later the peony leaves will give welcome shade to the primroses. The maturing foliage retains a pink tinge in the leaf stalks but the rounded lobes of the leaves become an attractive pale grey-green. The cupped flowers appear in late spring, earlier than those of most hybrid peonies, and last for two or three weeks. They are a tender shade of primrose-yellow, with a crown of golden stamens at the centre.

To my eye the pale yellow of the peony flower looks best in the company of blues and I would like to see it underplanted with bluebells or with the lovely shade-loving *Omphalodes cappadocica* with its bright caerulean eyes, or with *Lithodora* (syn. *Lithospermum*) 'Heavenly Blue'.

At the end of summer, the peony has another gift in store: the seedheads split to reveal brightly coloured berries which remain attached as the seedcase peels wide open. The mature berries are shiny black but the immature ones and those that have shrivelled are blood-red. This two-toned effect will stop you in your tracks.

● Height and spread to 90cm/36in. Peonies like rich, well-drained soil in sun or part-shade. The thick, fleshy roots are said to resent disturbance; left unmolested the plant may survive for decades. However, one method of propagation is by division of the roots in spring. Alternatively grow from seed, but plants will take four years to mature to flowering size. Zone 4

OTHER PEONIES TO GROW

***Paeonia officinalis* 'Rubra Plena'** The common cottage garden peony, with flowers that are fluffy deep crimson balls up to 15cm/6in in diameter. These appear fleetingly in early summer. Good, deeply cut dark green leaves. Height and spread to 60cm/24in. The tuberous roots are easily divided. There are pink and also white varieties, less attractive in my view than the common form. Zone 3

***Paeonia lactiflora* varieties** For centuries this species was an obsession with Chinese gardeners who bred countless varieties, ranging from whites through pinks to deep crimson. Some are single in form; some are exotic doubles. In many of the doubles the central anthers have mutated into numerous thin ribbons, usually of the same colour as the petals. Among the most sensational flowers are

Paeonia lactiflora 'Emperor of India'

Paeonia lactiflora 'Bowl of Beauty'

Paeonia lactiflora 'Barrymore'

Paeonia lactiflora 'Bridal Veil'

'Bowl of Beauty', with pink petals surrounding a central 'explosion' of cream. 'Colonel Heneage' has petals and central frills that are magenta throughout. 'Duchesse de Nemours' is frilly white and deeply scented. 'Bridal Veil' is pink with cream anthers. 'Barrymore' is a paler pink. 'Emperor of India' (sometimes called 'Empress') is perhaps the most exotic, with deep rose petals surrounding a central crown of burnished gold. Height and spread to 90cm/36in. Zone 3

Pulmonaria saccharata

LUNGWORT

Spotted leaves for ground cover, pink and blue flowers in early spring

The pulmonarias are among the earliest of the herbaceous plants to flower. They come soon after the first spring bulbs, the snowdrops, and in advance of all but the earliest of the daffodils. *Pulmonaria saccharata* gives an attractive bicoloured effect in the

bare borders of early spring. The flower buds open pink, but within a day or two they have changed to a pastel blue. The flower heads are a loose gathering of tubular flowers arranged on a short stalk rather in the manner of a cowslip.

Only when the flowers have dropped do the leaves reach any size. They are elliptical and pointed, soft and slightly furry to the touch. Their background colour is dark green, but they are mottled with silvery-grey spots to a very variable extent – in some plants the leaves have small spots while in others the patterns merge to give an almost entirely silver leaf.

This is a well-behaved plant which seeds itself readily but does not become unduly invasive. It makes good ground cover, especially under trees and shrubs where few plants can put up with the dim light. It is most effective under deciduous shrubs, such as philadelphus or weigela, as long as there is enough moisture. The pulmonaria flowers will give

A dual-purpose perennial. *Pulmonaria saccharata* makes a compact and colourful companion for narcissi in early spring (BELOW LEFT). By midsummer (BELOW RIGHT) decorative foliage has spread to cover the bare ground, with *Alchemilla mollis* behind it.

pleasure before the shrub's leaves appear and its leaves will provide continuing interest at ground level later.

• Height 23cm/9in, spread 45cm/18in. Grows in shade or part-shade, any soil. Propagate by seed or division. Zone 3

OTHER PULMONARIAS TO GROW

Pulmonaria angustifolia This species has narrow leaves without the variegated patterns found in *P. saccharata*, but there are several varieties with superior flower colour. These include *P. angustifolia azurea* and *P. angustifolia* 'Mawson's Blue', both of which have gentian-blue flowers, the latter with chocolate-coloured calyces. Zone 3

Pulmonaria officinalis rubra A lungwort with flowers of a deep salmon-pink – a colour that I personally find a little aggressive in the bare borders of early spring. I prefer *P. officinalis* 'Sissinghurst White', with pure white flowers. Both forms have spotted leaves, though they are not so richly marked as those of *P. saccharata*. Zone 3

Pulsatilla halleri

PASQUE FLOWER

Silvery foliage, lilac-coloured spring flowers, followed by seedheads in summer

The Pasque flower is lovely in all its parts. Tufts of foliage push above the ground in early spring and open to reveal fern-like leaves, covered with soft white hairs which give an overall silvery effect. The flowers follow soon. Resembling anemones, they are also covered with fine hairs which give them the texture of soft felt. They are lilac-coloured with a mass of yellow stamens at the centre. This plant is an asset to any rock garden or alpine bed in spring. It would

be difficult to imagine any plant of softer appearance, or more inviting to the touch.

When the petals drop, you should resist deadheading this plant, as it has another treat in store. The round seedheads are covered with hairy wisps which catch the light, rather like 'old man's beard', the seedheads of the wild clematis.

Pulsatilla vulgaris is a relation and looks very similar, although the flowers are more variable in colour, ranging from purple through pink to white.

• Height 23cm/9in, spread 30cm/12in. Like other alpines, it prefers a gritty, well-drained soil such as may be incorporated into a rockery, raised bed or sink garden. Zone 5

Pulsatilla halleri in spring

Pulsatilla halleri in summer

Salvia officinalis

SAGE

Ornamental foliage, summer flowers

As a cooking herb, sage has relatively limited uses, but it has great value as an ornamental plant, by virtue of its several varieties with distinctive leaf colour. The purple sage, *Salvia officinalis* 'Purpurascens', is perhaps the most useful. It has attractively soft, felty leaves, dull purple in young growth, becoming green and lighter in tone when mature. With young and old leaves on the same plant, the two-tone effect of the foliage is attractive in itself, so it is a bonus when spikes of purple flowers appear in summer. The purple sage makes an effective contrast with silver-leaved shrubs. I have seen it well used as an underplanting to a massive cardoon, *Cynara cardunculus*, and underplanted, in turn, by the low-growing, grey-leaved *Stachys byzantina* (syn. *S. lanata*).

Another lovely sage is the yellow-variegated form *S. officinalis* 'Icterina', the patterns on whose leaves are particularly subtle. Plant this beside the purple sage to make a contrast; the leaf shape and texture are the same, but the colours, yellow and purple, are at opposite ends of the spectrum. A third variety, *S. officinalis* 'Tricolor', has leaves with bolder variegation. Here the leaf edges are creamy white, the centres green, and the younger shoots are dabbed with pink. Less vigorous and less hardy than the other varieties, it looks a little sickly to my eye, but every gardener must follow his or her own taste.

● Height 60cm/24in, spread 90cm/36in. Originating in the Mediterranean, sage likes a sunny position in any well-drained soil. It looks most attractive as a young plant, and it can become woody after a year or two. For best results, then, prune back strongly in spring; there is a risk that the plant will not survive this treatment, in which case replace it with a young

plant. Propagate by cuttings. *S.o.* 'Purpurascens' and 'Icterina' are hardy to zone 8, 'Tricolor' to zone 9.

Salvia officinalis
'Purpurascens'

OTHER SAGES TO GROW

The genus *Salvia* is a vast and diverse one, with some seven hundred species, many of which are useful in the garden. Among those that qualify for this book, the following have very different virtues from each other, and from *S. officinalis*, although a certain family likeness can be detected in the shapes of the flowers of all sages.

Salvia sclarea in summer

Salvia sclarea This is a biennial plant. In summer tall and dramatic sprays of long-lived lavender-pink flowers surmount its broad, furry leaves. These flowers are surrounded by bracts of a matching lavender, creating an overall shimmering effect. Height 75cm/30in, spread 60cm/24in. Zone 6

Salvia uliginosa Flowering over a long period towards the end of summer, S. *uliginosa* has small flowers, but many of them, on tall, open sprays of height 1.5m/5ft. They are sky-blue and look marvellous in the company of the mauve *Verbena bonariensis*, which is about the same height. Unfortunately this salvia is rather tender and needs winter protection in many areas. Zone 8

Grown from seed in a shaped bed within a restored nineteenth-century garden, a clump of *Salvia horminum* displays its colour range of white and pink through purple. It is boldly underplanted with red and purple verbenas.

Salvia horminum (now correctly S. *viridis*) This sage has long-lived flowers consisting of brightly coloured bracts of white, red or blue. These keep their colour when dried, and so this makes a good plant for winter decoration. Height 45cm/18in, spread 25cm/10in. Grow as an annual, from seed.

Salvia patens A perennial with intensely blue flowers which appear for many weeks in late summer. Standing some 45cm/18in in height, with a spread of 30cm/12in, S. *patens* makes a valuable ingredient for an all-blue border. If you prefer a pale version, *S.p.* 'Cambridge Blue' is the one for you. This salvia is quite tender and will only survive the winter in mild areas. Zone 9

Salvia patens in late summer

Sedum 'Autumn Joy'

ICE-PLANT

Blue-green leaves from spring, flowers in autumn,
seedheads for winter

This perennial emerges from dormancy very early in
the spring, with fleshy blue-green leaf-buds appearing at the base of last year's flower stems. It then
proceeds to grow steadily and to look promising
throughout the summer months. Other border
perennials come and go – phlox, geraniums, cam-
panulas all reach maturity and decline as the sedum
plods on. Its fleshy leaves swell, and the plant forms
an attractive clump, but only in early autumn do the
flowers mature. In flower it retains its good compact
shape, and never becomes straggly unless forced to

compete with its neighbours for light. Coinciding with dahlias and Michaelmas daisies, the pink flower heads are flat and fluffy and are quite irresistible to butterflies. I have counted twenty tortoiseshell butterflies on a single plant.

Sedum 'Autumn Joy' (correctly called 'Herbst-freude') has the added virtue of ageing gracefully through the seasons. The subtle, slightly biscuit-pink flowers deepen in colour to a dull burgundy and the stems remain hard enough to stay upright through the winter. A clump of sedum looks magical with a covering of frost, and will provide interest in the winter garden until new growth begins at the base in spring.

• Height and spread 45cm/18in. Any soil, preferably in full sun. Propagate by division, but it will also seed itself. It is advisable to lift and divide plants each year in spring, or else they are liable to become bare at the centre. Zone 4

OTHER SEDUMS TO GROW

Sedum kamtschaticum 'Variegatum' A succulent for the rock garden, with striking cream-variegated foliage and a prostrate habit. The flower buds are red, opening to yellow star-shaped flowers. Height 15cm/6in, spread 50cm/20in. Zone 4

LEFT TO RIGHT *Sedum* 'Autumn Joy' makes a good rounded shape at the front of the border in midsummer. Hardy geraniums and roses dominate the scene, but they are over by early autumn when the sedum comes into its own. The shrub behind the sedum is *Berberis thunbergii* 'Rose Glow'. This gives good colour from spring to autumn but is bare in midwinter when the dried flower heads of the sedum are still excellent value, providing flat perches on which hoar frost settles.

Sedum spectabile 'Meteor'

Sedum spectabile One of the parents of *S.* 'Autumn Joy', of the same dimensions, with similar biscuit-pink flower heads. *S. spectabile* 'Carmen' and *S. spectabile* 'Meteor' have fluffier flower heads of a brighter pink. Zone 4

Sedum 'Ruby Glow' A sprawling plant of height 25cm/10in and spread 45cm/18in, with grey-blue succulent foliage and heads of rose-red flowers in late summer and lasting well into autumn. Makes a useful edging plant for an autumn border. Zone 4

Sedum 'Vera Jameson' A sedum with succulent purplish-bronze leaves and dark pink flowers in late summer. It has a prostrate habit, with a height of 20cm/8in over a spread of 50cm/20in. Zone 4

Sedum 'Ruby Glow'

Silybum marianum

OUR LADY'S MILK THISTLE

Variegated foliage in spring, thistle-like flowers
in summer

One plant above all others inspires curiosity among visitors to my garden. This is *Silybum marianum*, a highly decorated form of thistle that can be an annual or a biennial. Like most thistles, S. *marianum* has undulating leaves with barbarous spines along their edges. The feature that distinguishes this plant and earns it the enchanting name of 'Our Lady's milk thistle' is the pattern of silver veining on the leaves. In its early growth the plant forms a broad rosette (about 75cm/30in diameter) of leaves that appear to glitter with this silver decoration. I find its broad, horizontal presence in the spring border the perfect companion for the vertically oriented tulips, particularly pale pink ones, such as 'Angélique', and the whites, 'Purissima' and 'White Triumphator'.

Silybum marianum in spring, with *Centaurea montana*, violas, tulips and forget-me-nots

A word of warning though. Wonderful as it is in young growth, this plant becomes a hulking and aggressive monster. Within a few weeks the tight rosette opens up, branches and expands upwards to a height of 1.5m/5ft. You are faced with a hazard in your border, for its spines will penetrate your flesh as if you were made of butter. The stiff expanding leaves, up to 90cm/36in wide, will edge out the neighbouring plants. I have absolutely no qualms about heaving out this cuckoo in the nest, long before it reveals its unpleasant nature. Yet equally I have no hesitation in continuing to grow it, as I cherish its young beauty.

There remains the problem of propagation. *S. marianum* is very easy to grow from seed, but of course you can only obtain seed from a mature plant that has been allowed to flower. For this purpose I grow one plant hidden away in a corner of the garden, so that I can save seed for the coming year.

• Height and spread at maturity 1.5m/5ft. Sunny position, any soil. Propagate by seed. Seeds sown inside in early spring and planted out when big enough will flower the same year. To obtain a sizeable rosette by tulip time, plant the seeds straight into the ground in early autumn. Zone 6

Vinca major 'Variegata'

VARIEGATED PERIWINKLE

Variegated evergreen foliage for ground cover, with lilac summer flowers

The periwinkles make extremely useful ground cover – provided you do not put them with more fragile plants. The more delicate perennials will stand little chance against the thuggish advance of the vinca. This is a virtue when you have waste ground that you would like to see screened by foliage, but the periwinkle will not be appropriate for your more subtle planting schemes.

Vinca major 'Variegata'

There is a wide choice of periwinkles available, varying in their size of leaf and colour of flower. My own favourite is the large-leaved variegated form, which has lilac flowers in early summer. With its brightly patterned leaves it can bring a little light to a shady corner under trees. Personally, I find it effective in a raised bed above a terrace, where its long shoots trail over the side, finding no purchase for new roots in the stone slabs below. It will also soften the austerity of raised beds made from bricks or railway sleepers, and its great virtue is that it remains equally effective in winter. It is worth cutting the plant right back in spring as the new growth will look much neater than the old.

• This vinca is unfussy in its requirements – it will grow in any soil and is content in sun or shade. It puts out long shoots of mottled green leaves, edged with creamy yellow, that grow up to 1.2m/4ft long. Where a shoot tip meets the soil it will take root and so the plant will 'leapfrog' across the ground if it is left undisturbed. Wherever it takes root it makes a bushy growth of new shoots. Zone 8

Viola cornuta

HORNED VIOLET

Flowers from late spring to autumn

Here is a plant that will flower for you from late spring to autumn with hardly a pause for breath. Sometimes it will flower so persistently that it runs out of energy and dies of exhaustion. However, it will have produced so much seed beforehand that you will be very unlucky if a new generation does not spring up to take its place the following season.

Compared with its highly bred cousins the pansies, this species viola has flowers that are restrained in colour and modest in size. They are pure lilac without any patterning, and shaped like large and flattened violets. There is also a pure white form which comes true to seed. In the right conditions this viola is a prodigious performer, with a dense display of flowers which are constantly replaced, especially if you are able to dead-head the plants.

Viola cornuta is an ideal plant to line the edge of a border. It also looks good as an underplanting in the bare area under roses. The lilac hue associates well with the broken pinks and purples of old-fashioned roses such as *R.* 'Cardinal de Richelieu'.

• Makes a mound up to 40cm/15in high, spreading to 60cm/24in. It likes sun or part-shade, but is intolerant of dry conditions. Zone 6

Viola cornuta, planted under a gleditsia

INDEX

Page numbers in bold type refer to main entries

Zone chart
Approximate range of average annual minimum temperatures
1 below $-45°C/-50°F$
2 $-45°C/-50°F$ to $-40°C/-40°F$
3 $-40°C/-40°F$ to $-34°C/-30°F$
4 $-34°C/-30°F$ to $-29°C/-20°F$
5 $-29°C/-20°F$ to $-23°C/-10°F$
6 $-23°C/-10°F$ to $-18°C/0°F$
7 $-18°C/0°F$ to $-12°C/10°F$
8 $-12°C/10°F$ to $-7°C/20°F$
9 $-7°C/20°F$ to $-1°C/30°F$
10 $-1°C/30°F$ to $4°C/40°F$
11 above $4°C/40°F$

The hardiness zone ratings given for each plant suggest the approximate
minimum temperature a plant will tolerate in winter. However, this can
only be a rough guide. The hardiness of a plant depends on a great many
factors, including the depth of its roots, its water content at the onset of
frost, the duration of cold weather, the force of the wind, and the length
and heat of the preceding summer.

ACKNOWLEDGMENTS

AUTHOR'S ACKNOWLEDGMENTS

Rosemary Verey was an inspiration from the outset. Sue Dickinson was generous with advice on cultivation. I was very privileged to be able to call on Tony Lord, distinguished Editor of *The Plant Finder* for authentication of plant names.

At home, my tangled texts were patiently unravelled by Gillian Naish, Judy Dod and Carolyn McNab, who word-processed them and served them up to the publisher on a disk. On this my first venture into writing about gardening I count myself especially fortunate to have worked with Frances Lincoln's outstanding publishing team. Jo Christian has been the most painstaking of editors, so thorough and so self-effacing that she is bound to cut out this sentence unless I put my foot down. Serena Dilnot backed her up admirably, and Sandra Raphael meticulously compiled the index. On the design front, Louise Tucker and James Campus were very sensitive in the linking of text and pictures and were most tactful with an opinionated author.

My only disagreements have been with the photographer. Seeing us at work, people might think that we are inseparable. The truth is that we are firm rivals and it is my contention that his pictures distract people from reading my text.

PUBLISHERS' ACKNOWLEDGMENTS

The publishers would like to thank Joanna Chisholm, Margaret Crowther, Sarah Mitchell, Ray Rogers and Caroline Taylor for their help in the production of this book.

PHOTOGRAPHER'S ACKNOWLEDGMENTS

I am most grateful to the garden owners who have generously allowed me to take pictures in their gardens. They include the following:

Mr and Mrs Bill Baker; Mrs Gerda Barlow; Batsford Arboretum; Mrs Gwen Beaumont; M. Raymond Blanc; the late Humphrey Brooke; Mr & Mrs Martin Caroe; The Hon. C. & Mrs Cecil; Mr & Mrs J. Chambers; Mr & Mrs Leo Clark; Mrs Anne Dexter; Mr & Mrs Mike Elliott; Fibrex Nurseries; Mr & Mrs Thomas Gibson; Mr & Mrs Harry Hay; The Hon. Mrs E. Healing; Mr & Mrs David Hodges; Mr & Mrs John Hubbard; Lady Mary Keen; Mr C. Laikin; Mr & Mrs David Langton; Mr & Mrs L. Lauderdale; Miss Joan Loraine; Mr & Mrs Peter Maclaren; Mr & Mrs Ralph Merton; Mr & Mrs Jeremy Naish; Dr Julia Trevelyan Oman; Norrie and Sandra Pope; Mrs J.H. Robinson & John Brookes; Lord & Lady Saye and Sele; Mr & Mrs Kurt Schoenenberger; Mrs Shuker & Mrs Pollitt; Dr James Smart; Ron Spice; Rosemary Verey; Mr & Mrs Robin Wade; Mr & Mrs Geoff Walton; Mr & Mrs Whittington; Mr & Mrs John Williams.

Horticultural Consultant   Tony Lord
Editor   Jo Christian
Art Editor   Louise Tucker
Designer   James Campus
Picture Editor   Anne Fraser
Production   Adela Cory
Editorial Director   Erica Hunningher
Art Director   Caroline Hillier
Production Director   Nicky Bowden